Great Lakes Folklore
Legends of the Five Sisters

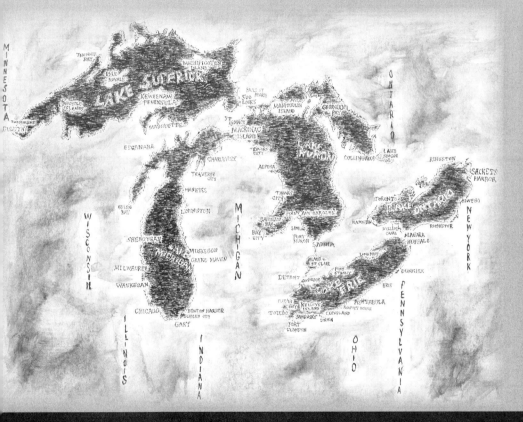

Charles Cassady, Jr.

4880 Lower Valley Road • Atglen, PA 19310

Dedication

For Ed Ville.
Safe passage, Brother Ed.

Schiffer Books are available at special discounts for bulk purchases for sales promotions or premiums. Special editions, including personalized covers, corporate imprints, and excerpts can be created in large quantities for special needs. For more information contact the publisher:

Published by Schiffer Publishing, Ltd.
4880 Lower Valley Road
Atglen, PA 19310
Phone: (610) 593-1777; Fax: (610) 593-2002
E-mail: Info@schifferbooks.com

For the largest selection of fine reference books on this and related subjects,
please visit our website at **www.schifferbooks.com**.
We are always looking for people to write books on new and related subjects.
If you have an idea for a book,
please contact us at *proposals@schifferbooks.com*.

This book may be purchased from the publisher.
Please try your bookstore first.
You may write for a free catalog.

Other Schiffer Books By The Author:

Paranormal Mississippi River: An Illustrated Encyclopedia, 978-0-7643-3898-4, $24.99

Cleveland Ghosts, 978-0-7643-3002-5, $14.99

Paranormal Great Lakes: An Illustrated Encyclopedia, 978-0-7643-3295-1, $14.99

Copyright © 2013 by Charles Cassady, Jr.

Cover image by Paul Wunderle
Text and images by author unless otherwise noted

Library of Congress Control Number: 2013945105

Designed by Mark David Bowyer
Type set in Rosemary Roman / NewBaskerville BT

ISBN: 978-0-7643-4480-0
Printed in the United States of America

Contents

Acknowledgements

I must thank my editor, Dinah Roseberry, for patience in entrusting me with this project and tolerating my suggestions and stallings where anyone else might well commit mutiny. Other tidings of gratitude go to Rich Norgard, for his research and advice on the convict ship *Success*; Georgann and Michael Wachter for generosity, wreck information and Powerpoint presentation skills I will never equal; Elaine Hinton for a memorable tour of Fairport Harbor; Robert Dean Wells in the Chicago Bureau; Lois Beardslee for contributions, directions, and hard-won wisdom; George McDougall Jr. for dark family secrets; Gerard Altoff for Battle of Lake Erie intelligence; Laura Shields and the Old Lighthouse Museum of the Michigan City Historical Society; Mike Fletcher for helping navigate the trails of missing submarines; Patricia Gruse Harris, for sharing what she knew of Lodner Darvonitis Phillips and his family. More thanks go out to Paul Wunderle, Lucy McKernan, Erik Schroeder and the ensemble of the Lookingglass Theatre, Chip Karpus, Caleb Pifer, Charles Cassady Sr., Dr. Melanie Higgins, Sean Ley, Richard Novak, and the Chicago Historical Society; Virginia Warnke and the Owens Group, especially Kim Moss and Laura Ambro.

Introduction

I n a different life, not so very long ago, I kept busy and made a subsistence living as a freelance entertainment reporter in the Cleveland, Ohio area. At one point, my alternative-weekly newspaper – it still existed at the time – sent me on an assignment more interesting than most. Two young actors, Richard Wilson and Emma Booth, had flown all the way from their native Australia to be goodwill ambassadors for *Clubland*, a motion-picture comedy-drama in which they costarred. And I had the luck to be assigned the interview.

The performers happened to be lodged at a plush downtown Cleveland hotel that functioned as an adjunct to the main reason many international visitors come to Cleveland, the sprawling Cleveland Clinic hospital complex. As an index of the prominence of the Cleveland Clinic, there was another special event happening on this world-class medical campus the very day of my afternoon question-and-answer interrogation. The President of the United States was giving an address.

While I did indeed study Journalism at a major university in order to place myself in the proverbial center-of-things, very little adventure ever transpired in my post-graduate career. Accordingly, I overdid it that day. For any eventuality at the Clinic, I packed a second-hand press photographer's Nikon digital SLR camera I had purchased, plus one of my best telephoto lenses; a compact tape recorder; a customized hat that said "PRESS" on it; and an oversized camera bag with "MEDIA" affixed to the strap – just so my intentions would not be misunderstood. All I might have lacked was a foreign correspondent's trenchcoat, a thin notebook with a pencil, and the right kind of face – preferably Cary Grant's or Gregory Peck's, circa 1940s. In the event that some terrible calamity happened coincident with the Chief Executive's presence, I would be a mobile news-gathering apparatus, Johnny-on-the-spot.

I parked a good distance away from the Clinic's center and made my trek on foot. Security details had evidently kept much of the traffic blocked off, and the Clinic was more peaceable than I would have expected. And nobody challenged me or attempted to verify that my large black "MEDIA" bag or long black coat did indeed hold benign news gear and not something more dire. I must admit I had a secondary motivation in attiring myself; I was curious to see if any Secret Service on the perimeter of the Clinic would judge me a suspicious character and investigate. But no such thing happened as I made my way to the hotel. Either I was too far from the President's location to be considered any remote threat...or federal agents instantly recognized me from my years on the local alt-journalism scene. This latter was extremely unlikely.

When I reached the hotel suite in which the Australians were ensconced, I did frighten one dignitary: actress Emma Booth. She saw my Nikon equipment and assumed I had expected to perpetrate a formal celebrity photo shoot. She feared she was not looking her most glamorous and wanted no paparazzi antics. I had to assure her that lugging such an arsenal around was standard practice for Charles Cassady, ace freelance reporter/reviewer, and that no lens need be unsheathed if it vexed her. Diplomatically, I withheld that my photographic firepower was not intended for the actors, but for any potential riots, disorder, or assassination attempts that might have unfolded with the Presidential entourage so tantalizingly nearby.

I don't believe she quite trusted me. Nonetheless, as a trouper she conducted her scheduled interview with this annoying apparition that hailed from...what newspaper exactly? And young Mr. Wilson was quite affable and forthcoming, although, if memory serves, the two of them and their handlers occasionally broke away from the session to crane their necks out the window for signs of the Presidential motorcade with full police escort.

Directly after our interview and the lifting of security around the block, the pair were to be rushed to the airport and onto the next major city in which *Clubland* had a playdate. I felt I owed the two young Australians a piece of trivia that might appeal to them as symbolic token of thanks, and so I asked, did they know that not far from here, to the west in shallow waters of Lake Erie, is where the wreck of the *Success* is?

No, they had not heard that. Richard Wilson seemed particularly interested (or was a very good actor). Yes, I continued, the *Success*. Not much left to see, since she burned down to the waterline. But depending on your airliner's flight path, as you leave Cleveland you may be going right over the spot.

The *Success* was an ancient teakwood sailing ship that earned legendary status in Australia, as a vintage prison hulk from the 19th-century days of the Outback gold rush. In later years, retired from penal work, she transformed into a sort of museum – though chamber-of-horrors might have been a better appellation, as foreign torture-devices and yarns of violence and horror became a part of her unique appeal. As a morbid attraction for paying customers, she hosted numerous Australian curiosity seekers before literally traveling the world in the late 1800s and early 1900s. And she had come around the planet to her final rest here, in fresh water, just off Sandusky.

She was once practically a household name. Now few outside the circle of Great Lakes history buffs and wreck divers speak of her. But I hope that small echo of Australia's past made the two young ambassadors of Antipodal showbiz feel slightly more compensated as they went on their mandatory press circuit. Perhaps their Cleveland stopover would always live in their minds for a sitting president's proximity – but I had to give them that one extra dose of serendipity; here is where the *Success'* epic came to its end.

The *Success* is part of my stock-file I have come to carry with me, tales gleaned since childhood by fresh-water osmosis and reading the storytellers of yesterday and today who made the Great Lakes their specialty. Authors like Dwight Boyer, Frederick Stonehouse, Dana Thomas Bowen, Walter Havighurst and others. Life near the Great Lakes, or any main-traveled seaways, enhances one's capacity for stories indeed.

Once it was my privilege to interview Linda Greenlaw. She was a novelty, a New England female fishing-boat skipper and a supporting player in the real-life drama of ocean-water heroism and loss among mid-Atlantic fishermen that became Sebastian Junger's book *The Perfect Storm*. After the popularity of Junger's saga with readers worldwide, publishers were delighted to find that Linda Greenlaw could also tell a story. And tell it well. They signed her to produce her own anthology of nautical observations, humor, memoir, even a ghost story or two. And when her fishing season came to an end and she had the time, Linda Greenlaw wrote another book, and another. She segued into fiction, writing nautical mystery novels as well. And thus did Linda Greenlaw become only the latest of a number of authors with the tides in their blood.

Joseph Conrad and Jack London were two sailors-turned-authors. The Dane Peter Freuchen achieved renown as "the vagrant Viking," a world-traveling seaman and explorer and oceanic authority who, given a proper trident and crown, would have possessed quite a resemblance to King Neptune. Oceanographer Jacques Cousteau was a best-selling author before becoming identified with a long-running series of televised documentaries.

Thor Heyerdahl was an archaeologist with a controversial theory that the South Pacific islands of Polynesia had been settled by ancient explorers from South America. To prove this was even possible – and after a consultation with Peter Freuchen – he and five crewmen built what they envisioned as an aboriginal-style seafaring raft of wood and reeds (built without nails) to sail the 4,300 nautical miles themselves. Heyerdahl's resulting book *Kon-Tiki* topped the bestseller lists in several languages. It inspired a long career of adventure writing for Heyerdahl, if not acceptance of his theories of history.

Daniel Gallery entered the US Naval Academy at age 16. In a distinguished WWII career, during his action against German submarine fleets, he conceived in an audacious plan to capture a U-boat intact, an operation he was able to accomplish off the coast of Africa in 1944. Near the end of the war he was given command of an aircraft carrier. Afterwards, Lt. Col. Gallery authored several volumes of naval fiction and nonfiction. Edward "Ned" Beach was a US Navy submarine instructor and later commander, who served in the Battle of Midway and earned medals throughout the Atlantic and Pacific. In between wartime and peacetime duties, he was a Naval Aide to President Eisenhower. Following the lead of his own father, a Navy man and author in his own right, Beach published prolifically, including the classic novel of underwater warfare, *Run Silent Run Deep*.

Alistair MacLean, a best-selling adventure novelist whose name was accompanied on book covers by the two-word description "Master Storyteller," was a young seaman in the Royal Navy. Pursuing a writing career after VE day, he drew upon his nautical experience (with input from his brother Ian, a Master Mariner) to pen the popular *HMS Ulysses*, first in a series of top-selling action-thrillers.

And there are many more. But I am most taken with the background of Tristan Jones, a specialist in nonfiction "yarns." He was literally born on his father's boat and logged an estimated 345,000 miles, voyaging from the Antarctic to the Amazon to the Red Sea to Tahiti, before settling down to pour out memoir after memoir of adventure. In a 1979 essay for *Writers Digest*, he evoked his upbringing in Llangereth, Wales, and how a sailor named Cadell Rum came back from his periodic world travels to regale the community.

> Cadell talked and took us to where the groaning bergs calved off the glaciers, or up a dark alley rife with skullduggery in Bombay or Madagascar. When Cadell told a tale everyone, even Mister-Jeffreys-Geography, the English schoolteacher, stared enchanted.

Storytelling, it has been observed, makes us human; Joan Didion called it essential for human survival. And the men and women of the sea, it seems, have a stronger claim to that part of humanity than most. It may be the hours spent in isolation, on watch, at the wheel or the tiller in calm weather, or on the cloistered duty of manning a lighthouse, with only words to entertain. Peter Freuchen wrote it was a lonely post at Ultima Thule, in Greenland, that served as his muse, sending his mind at work dwelling on the sea before him and all that was stowed in its history. Of course, it has also been the nature of a sailor's life to travel so far, see so much, and have the reason to remember. And speak the lore in a richness of language that would humble an educated English schoolteacher.

For my own part, I never served on a ship or spent a great amount of time on a shore that was seldom more than several miles from where I grew up. I regret that now. A closer proximity to the waves – and a farther one from classrooms – might have made me a better storyteller, I think.

Holding twenty percent of the world's fresh water, my Great Lakes are huge lakes, veritable inland seas rivaled only by the Caspian Sea in Russia and Lake Victoria in Africa. Ohio author and historian L.E. Hopkins wrote of entertaining a visitor from Louisiana who, looking upon the expanse of Lake Erie, could not accept this was not really part of the ocean until dipping a finger in the water and checking for brine.

If my brief Australian friends, had they walked to the Cleveland shoreline... would they have sought similar physical proof?

The vastness of the Great Lakes, as seen from Benton Harbor, Michigan...

...and Marblehead, Ohio

The Great Lakes are often called the Inland Seas, or another poetical synonym applied: the Five Sisters – meaning Lakes Superior, Michigan, Huron, Erie, and Ontario. This latter designation ignores the smaller Lake St. Clair and a preference by some to distinguish Lake Huron as really two lakes, its northern shore of Georgian Bay a separate body partially breakwalled off from the rest of Huron by a sequence of huge islands. In successive eras these Great Lakes have borne Indians, explorers, immigrants, bandits, miners, warriors, and entrepreneurs.

And stories and storytellers. For, like other seas, waters of the Great Lakes are awash with great tales they inspired.

Stories have come from the folklore of the native people who preceded the Europeans by centuries. They have come from the early narratives of the pioneering settlers and explorers. They have come from the wars and intrigues over expanding new territories. They have come from the struggles against rain, ice, wind, waves, and human error that beset any mariner. They have come from the misadventures, desires, fears, and fantasies of those who make a home on or near the water.

I myself did not seek to make a living connected with the Great Lakes. As previously mentioned, I attended a pricey, landlocked college and was dutifully, dubiously "educated" in the technique of reportage. I do wonder if a different career path had presented itself, one more maritime in nature – and had I been open-minded enough to try it – then perhaps the learning experience would have made me a far better storyteller than those classes in upstate New York sitting under sterile fluorescent lighting.

So I do possess a reservoir of Great Lakes maritime stories, mysteries, myths, folklore, and legends. I bring them out on special occasions, as I did for Richard Wilson and Emma Booth.

Allow me to present you with a collection now. May they take you places you have never been, or show you things you had not considered. There is a famous allegorical painting of the Renaissance, of King Neptune offering Venice the riches of the sea. I hope this book offers you a sea of riches – an Inland Sea of stories.

—Charles Cassady Jr.
Seven Hills, Ohio 2012

A fanciful illustration of the Griffin sailing into oblivion, perhaps – as certain legends claim – to the beat of a mystical omen, the Ottawa Drum. *An India-ink rendering by author Charles Cassady Jr.*

Flight of the *Griffin*

In Which We Learn of the Fabled Griffin. *Often Called the Oldest Great Lake Shipwreck, She in Truth Missed by a Fraction that Dubious Honor. Ambitions of Rene Robert Cavalier, Sieur de La Salle, his Motley Crew, and his Ignoble Fate. Perils of Setting Sail to the Pounding of the Ottawa Drum, a Blaspheming Viking Giant at the Rudder. Confusions Regarding Bleached Timbers and Bones on Yon Beach and in Eldritch Caves Hereabouts.*

I t is with the *Griffin* that most Great Lakes popular folklore begins. The first ship on the Inland Seas. The first shipwreck on the Lakes. The first "ghost ship" on the Lakes.

All of these firsts must be qualified, heavily. Boats did travel the Great Lakes well before the *Griffin*, well before the white man. The native Indian tribes around the lakes – the Iroquois, Algonquin, Mohawk, Oneida, Menominee, Senaca, Oneida, Ojibwe (Chippewa), and others, establishing trade routes and raiding-party passages for their dugouts, canoes, and pirogues. It was under the Ojibwe, according to historian Henry Beston, that the birch-bark canoe reached its apex. It was not an invention native to the Great Lakes, but generations of Ojibwe craftsmen had honed it to perfection. "Strong, well-made, capable of carrying heavy loads, yet easy to portage, the Chippewa model like the covered wagon is part of the history of this continent." The *voyageurs*, those hardy French fur traders who befriended the Indians and paddled the Great Lakes as well as Canada's networks of rivers, adopted the birchbark canoe as their own.

But the oral traditions and tales of the Great Lakes Indians come down to us haphazardly, often transcribed by the learned Jesuit missionaries who sought conversion to Christianity for the so-called "savage." With the attendant religious and cultural bias, the white men penned the tribal legends in their own words, often reinforcing their ingrained prejudices and agendas. Which leaves us to wonder, how accurate are these second-hand sagas?

There is, for one good example, the Portes des Mortes Strait linking Lake Michigan and Green Bay, between the northern tip of the peninsula of Door County, Wisconsin, and the Potawatomi cluster of islands. In Anglicized translations of the French, the strait carries the dire name Door of Death, or Death's Door.

Most explanations for the singularly ominous name describe a 17th-century war between the Winnebagos and the Potawatomis. Discovering a plan by the Potawatomi to attack their camp, the Winnebago lit false signal fires luring the enemy to a treacherous point on the shore. There the Winnebago warriors could rain arrow and tomahawk upon the war canoes below, as the hapless Potawatomi were dashed against the rocks by stormy seas. But then the Winnebagos, knowing that the Potawatomi village of women and children had been left undefended, took to the lake themselves to launch an attack. The strait, however, remained merciless, showing no favor, and this counter-attack fleet of warriors and their birchbarks also disappeared in the churning waves. The area, thus, struck fear into the Indians as a literal "door to death."

Or did it? White Europeans were not averse to making up such yarns; all the better if they portrayed the indigenous inhabitants whose lands they coveted in the most uncivilized light possible. There is also an amusing allegation the French merchant-colonists gave Death's Door Strait its name as pure propaganda, a verbal scarecrow as it were, something frightful enough to dissuade English traders from utilizing the route.

It was under the French flag, that the *Griffin* sailed, as a ship of commerce, conquest, and conversion. Something stronger and more substantial than any canoe, pirogue, or any European vessel that had ever sailed before her. Though a merchant ship, she carried light cannon in the manner of a man o'war, and one might conjecture that her construction was as symbolic as it was necessary, to demonstrate that expansion-minded Europeans planned to master these inland seas as much has they had the oceans.

She was initiated at the behest of Rene Robert Cavalier, Sieur de La Salle, a mouthful of aristocracy, often shortened to La Salle in the many narratives about him. Would French influence have prevailed more strongly in the future United States than it did, his fame may have reached the household-name status of Lewis and Clark. In the early-history lessons in schoolhouses along the Mississippi River he remains something of Christopher Columbus figure.

Born in Rouen, France, in 1643, La Salle was educated as a Jesuit and had a missionary brother working in Canada and businessman cousin in Montreal. Feeling a pull towards adventure and exploration for France, La Salle crossed the Atlantic to land in "New France" (eastern Canada) in 1667, where he erected his own fort and trading post and became a colonial figure of considerable influence.

In those days, the Great Lakes were themselves dubbed by the French by different names that the ones now emblazoned on charts. Lake Frontenac was the name carried by the present-day Lake Ontario, and it was the family moniker of the influential Count Frontenac, who was La Salle's patron. Lake Erie, meanwhile, was Lake Conty. The linguistic sound-a-like Lake Condé, confusingly enough, was Lake Superior. Lake Orleans was Lake Huron. Lake Dauphin (or, depending on the region, Lake Joseph) was Lake Michigan. Rather surprisingly, given all this rebranding, Lake St. Clair has remained Lake St. Clair ever since La Salle's explorations.

La Salle, like many others, thought that China itself lay somewhere to the west beyond these great waters, and with it, more opportunities for missionary work – inextricably linked to commercial prospects and territorial acquisitions. While the French fur-trading *voyageurs* used birchbark canoes to make their seasonal forays (often under incredibly harsh conditions) up and down the New Word's many rivers, a Great Lakes trade route – perhaps one leading to the lands and storehouses of the Great Khan – required something more formidable, like a commercial cargo-ship. Canoes could be carried aboard this vessel and be used to board her as she lay at anchor off the isolated outposts and growing towns along these freshwater seas.

And thus the *Griffin* was built. Only...not just yet. Here is where most storytellers and legend-makers get it wrong or simply ignore the fact that at least two, and possibly four, wooden vessels are known to have struck out upon the lakes before the *Griffin*. They were a pair of two-masted sloops, the first in a flotilla envisioned by LaSalle and his partners. Each was about forty feet long and probably carried minimal adornments. There is even some doubt as to whether one had a name. The other barque did, however. The forty-ton ship was known as the *Frontenac*.

She was to figure in an expedition of men, priests and supplies following along the north coast of Lake Ontario/Frontenac, headed for the Niagara River. La Salle had brought along with him an enterprising acquaintance, the Franciscan Friar Father Louis Hennepin, whose role in the saga of the *Griffin* is a crucial but problemantical one. Fr. Hennepin would write memoir after memoir of his adventures in the New World, and modern-day historians do not consider him the most reliable of narrators. Nonetheless, it is largely due to his accounts that we know even as much about the *Frontenac* and the *Griffin* as we do.

The sloops launched on November 18, 1678. November has since become infamous as the necessary cut-off month of the shipping season on the Great Lakes, as the teeth of winter close on the region, rendering the waters unfit for all but Coast Guard icebreakers until the spring. To squeeze in one last run of commercial cargo, to make one last portage deadline before the year's end, generations of merchant vessels have tried to outrun the grim advance of ice and snow fronts with the same recklessness that a motorist might attempt to cross railroad tracks across a road despite the danger of an approaching locomotive. And so often the results are similarly fatal. The "gales of November" on the Great Lakes are infamous as ship-killers, as the newly built *Frontenac* was to demonstrate.

The pilot of La Salle's *Frontenac*, later to serve in the same capacity on board the *Griffin*, is a shadowy man who has come down through history mostly filtered through the very unfavorable opinion of Fr. Hennepin. Our outsized view of him may be completely inaccurate, yet it would feed the legends to come in a manner that befits the cliche "larger than life." In La Salle's records, the man was known as Lucas, and he was stated to have been of gigantic stature, perhaps near to seven feet in height. There is some question as to whether he was even French or a Scandinavian, a Viking-like character also called Luke the Dane, portrayed by the friar as having a black temper worthy of a Norse pagan marauder. But it is quite possible this was simply a misreading of his full name, Lucas Daré, a legitimate Frenchman's moniker.

More is known about La Salle's most trusted officer, Henri de Tonty, a dashing young Italian-descended soldier who, during a battle in Sicily, lost most of his left hand in a grenade explosion. Tonty had the mangled stump fitted with a iron claw – the literal hook-hand of so much piratical imagery – and with this prothesis he was said to be both an adept worker and a formidable fighter in single combat.

Lucas Daré/Dane was installed as the pilot of the *Frontenac*. The nameless first ship left to voyage along the north shore of the 'future' Lake Ontario. Fleeing a storm into a river channel, the ship was soon frozen in place with the falling temperatures. Her crew had to chop their way through to the open water to continue their journey, finally arriving at the westernmost end of the lake, at the eastern shore of the Niagara River. There, in the midst of potentially unfriendly Seneca Indian lands, the men erected a stockade fort at what would prove a strategically important trading and military route.

La Salle was determined to take the *Frontenac* to inspect the encampment, supply it with additional provisions and ship-building materials, and do his best with gifts and tribute to placate the Senecas. A historic meeting and trading session took place between the voyagers of the *Frontenac* and the Indians on Christmas Day, 1678. La Salle also sought the blessings of the Senecas for further plans to construct a even bigger ship at Niagara, a "big canoe." But in the meanwhile disaster struck the *Frontenac*.

One version says that the ship became becalmed in early January, 1679. La Salle left instructions for Lucas to take the *Frontenac* either to Niagara or the Genessee River, depending on the prevailing winds. Instead, the pilot and the crew abandoned the frigid ship to build a fire and sleep on shore, where they awoke to find that a wind, during the night, had snapped the anchorage lines and sent the unmanned boat smashing to pieces against the shore. Fr. Hennepin's account claims, rather vaguely, that Lucas and another sailor had disagreed on the proper route to reach Niagara and "the barque was unfortunately cast away" against the south shore of the lake, with no loss of life and minimal provisions taken off her. Either way, the *Frontenac* was no more, and Tonty later attempted without success to salvage what he could from the wreck.

Unhappy (especially with the maladroit performance of Lucas) but undaunted, La Salle ordered construction started on his "big canoe," with what remained from the *Frontenac* calamity or could be fabricated in situ. The work teams cut white-oak timber on the spot for what would turn out to be the *Griffin*.

Compared to the lakeboats of later centuries, she would seem absurdly small. Yet nothing of her size and intention had ever breached these waters before. La Salle's *Griffin* was designed as a sixty-ton barque, about seventy feet long and sixteen feet wide. Her keel was laid personally by La Salle in early 1679 near Cayuga Creek on Lake Erie near Niagara Falls, amidst a small complex of cabins, a launch ramp and a blacksmith's forge built around her. Besides the function of her seven light cannon and generous cargo hold, she was distinguished by a carved emblem, lion-headed and eagle-winged on the prow, a mythological chimera that was the family crest and trademark of Count Frontenac. As one boat had already borne the name *Frontenac*, this one would instead carry the nomenclature of the creature – *Griffin*, or, in a more properly French spelling variation in other chronicles, *Le Griffon*.

By late May, 1679, she underwent a trial launch into Cayuga Creek and a blessing by Fr. Hennepin. La Salle now arranged his fortunes on the new ship as a supply vessel, and perhaps more, as the oaken embodiment of his resolve to persevere and prosper in this wilderness. Word of the loss of the *Frontenac* had spread and demoralized the scatterings of La Salle's men along the lakeshore.

Some feared La Salle had given up and abandoned them, while La Salle's creditors impounded his property in the embryonic ports. La Salle traveled across miles of wilderness to repair his damaged reputation; tried to install what non-mutinous employees and missionaries he could; and he personally set sail with the *Griffin* on August 7, 1679, on her first voyage of trading.

Once again, Lucas Daré was the pilot, and Tonty and Hennepin were also on board, as the ship sailed into Lake Erie, periodically firing the cannon to announce La Salle's approach in the most imperious fashion possible. Even so, they sometimes encountered only fleeing or idle remnants of the men who had been sent ahead on foot to establish trade beach-heads. The deserters had either lost confidence in La Salle or lost their nerve in dealing with potentially dangerous Indians without the cannon and muskets of a man o'war to back them up.

On the northern shore of Lake Erie, La Salle was fortunate enough to have descriptions of the terrain from a previous pair of missionaries; thus the *Griffin* avoided grounding on what would later be known as Long Point, a treacherous, narrow peninsula of shallows and shoals jutting out into lake. Long Point would be a notorious snare for unwary sailing ships.

On the way past what would later become the city of Detroit, La Salle named Lake St. Clair, having sailed around it on the feast day of that same saint. An arduous passage into Lake Orleans (Huron) led to the *Griffin* being battered by a late-August storm so violent that everyone aboard knelt in prayer for their deliverance – all except Lucas, wrote Fr. Hennepin. Lucas cursed and raged instead at having ever left saltwater behind. Hennepin called him the "godless pilot."

The *Griffin* went on to sail through Sault St. Marie. Impressively attired in his scarlet tunic and plumed hat, La Salle made a highly visible tour of French settlements around present-day Lake Michigan into September. Here, in the vicinity of Green Bay, Wisconsin, on September 18, he parted ways with the ship. It had been La Salle's master plan to forge ahead overland to the land of the Illinois Indian tribes – roughly, Peoria – and begin to establish trade routes along the Mississippi River. The *Griffin*, meanwhile, was to return to Fort Niagara in western New York, with her cargo hold laden with the thousands of pounds of pelts La Salle had acquired, the treasure on which his future enterprises relied. The trusted Sieur de Tonty, as Fr. Hennepin called him, also did not sail on the *Griffin*. He had been sent behind, on the route from which the ship had just come, to arrest two deserters at Sault St. Marie, and he would not return until November. So five crewman (and, by some accounts, a boy) and pilot Lucas Daré were given the formidable task of manning the *Griffin* alone for the return voyage.

Historians have surmised that additional crew members were to have boarded en route, before the hardest navigational hazards loomed. We will never know. After firing her cannon one last time, and sailing with a favorable light west winds, the *Griffin* – passing not far from that same area forebodingly dubbed as "Portes des Mortes" for its bloody history in Indian lore – receded from view. And then just disappeared entirely from history.

It would be some weeks, as La Salle followed on land, that he realized the *Griffin* had not made the expected rendezvous points, and she had effectively vanished. Yes, the *Griffin* had disappeared, becoming the first Great Lakes "ghost ship," a lost vessel whose exact fate is unknown.

Fr. Hennepin's writings on the end of the *Griffin* contained this rumor, that the ship was at anchor in "Lake Dauphin" when local Indians advised Lucas Daré to seek shelter from an approaching storm. Instead, the "godless pilot" on whose watch the *Frontenac* had met her end, defiantly sailed into rough weather, dooming the ship and all aboard her. For his part La Salle, in the winter of 1680, despaired of the furs and supplies he had trusted to the safety of belowdecks, and he trekked overland back east to find out any word of the ship. But there was none, save that the ship had apparently never even reached as far as Sault St. Marie.

Only once did a rumor reach La Salle's ears that may have provided a clue. In 1683, a young Indian given to La Salle as a slave told him of an impressively tall white man being held captive by native tribes far inland, west of the Mississippi. The tall man and four other white men were in loaded canoes, headed towards the territory of the Sioux, when they were captured. All but the giant were tortured and killed (and, if the informant was correct, cannibalized). La Salle could never verify the rumor, but it suggested one scenario – that pilot and crew, without the supervision and authority of Tonty, had mutinied, perhaps scuttling the *Griffin* and taking the cargo for themselves, only to be captured by a hostile tribe during their getaway.

If factual, this would not be the last time at all that La Salle was betrayed. In 1687, after an epic but troubled career exploring down the Mississippi River and claiming much of the Louisiana territory for France, he was shot in the head and robbed of his belongings – including his famous scarlet tunic – by one of his own men in the swamps of Texas. Henri de Tonty would die later of yellow-fever in a Louisiana colony. Fr. Louis Hennepin would return to Europe and regale readers with volumes of writings extolling and embroidering his travels in the New World.

And the *Griffin*?

Great Lakes author and newspaper reporter Dwight Boyer considered it very suspicious that Lucas Daré had apparently agreed to lead the *Griffin* back east with a ridiculously small crew. Perhaps, wrote Boyer, Lucas never seriously intended to finish the trip after all, but helped himself to the precious cargo with his co-conspirators, and let the *Griffin* perish in the water just as the *Frontenac* had.

Or perhaps poor seamanship had ended the *Griffin's* career. The theory has also been advanced that the same Indians who claimed the pilot had ignored their storm warning were in fact, brigands, who had attacked the undermanned vessel, overpowered the crew and seized its precious cargo of pelts; thus they told of a tragic storm and ship foundering as their cover story.

It has been noted sardonically that if one were to gather all the valuable Holy-relic slivers of wood allegedly to have been recovered from the True Cross, the sum total of the frauds would be enough timber for a good-sized forest. The same may be said of the first "Great Lakes ghost ship."

A 19th-century engraving depicts the destruction of a sailing ship by storm and rocks.

There is no shortage of wrecks around the Great Lakes, owing perhaps to an old maritime superstition (never apparently respected when there is money to be made from salvage) that the hulk of a beached ship, her curving timbers like the ribs of some giant animal, should be left undisturbed, lest back luck befall whoever disrupts the boat's final rest. Cris Kohl enumerated fifteen different claims for locations where wrecks or fragments of wrecks purporting to be the *Le Griffon* were found, the earliest dating to an 1848 Buffalo newspaper letter alleging, frustratingly, a discovery of relics four decades before, in sand around Hamburg, New York. The remains included rusted cannon with French inscriptions.

Some detective work by a late 19th-century historian, however, concluded that the guns came from a British warship that stranded much later. The cannon may well have been French, as it was the habit of the British to confiscate such weapons. This archaeological mistake would recur again and again in the long history of *Griffin*-hunting. Then there were the recent-vintage shipwrecks passed off as the remnants of the *Griffin* to gain attention and publicity.

Manitoulin Island, the largest lake island in the world, is a scenic, irregular mass of land in Lake Huron's North Channel. It is seventy-five miles long and forms a boundary between Lake Huron and Georgian Bay – practically turning Georgian Bay into a Great Lake all on its own. At the Mississagi Straits, at the western end of Manitoulin, stories persisted for generations that an ancient shipwreck lay here, known primarily to the Indians, who would occasionally recover artifacts from it. The lead used as caulking was particularly prized (to recycle into bullets), and, in 1877, the section of the wreck above the water was simply burned, all the better to sift through the ashes and recover most of the soft metal. Amidst the ashes, an old-timer later remembered, were metal rods that might have served to ram powder and shot into archaic cannon.

Nearby on Manitoulin Island in the 1890s, goes the tale, a lighthouse-keeper and occasional ship-builder named Albert Cullis and his assistant were prospecting for mast timber near where the wreck had been burned and chased a rabbit into a hole. Digging after the animal, they were astonished to break through to a large cave in the rocks. Inside were skeletons – one of them being of particularly large stature, such a Goliath in proportions that the jawbone fit neatly over the face of one of the living explorers. Also in the cave were gold, artifacts, and coins, suggesting French origin for the bodies, though another skeleton was wrapped in birchbark, possibly a later Indian burial. Subsequent searches turned up a second cave with more human remains – six dead in all, with further artifacts.

It was circumstantial evidence for believers that this was the crew of the *Griffin*, with the giant Lucas, and that La Salle's ship was the selfsame ancient wreck with the archaic lead caulking that lay in the Mississagi Strait. Some sort of mutiny or desertion – and perhaps an Indian attack – might have occurred. The relics and bones, especially the skulls, were kept as souvenirs by Cullis and his friends as conversation pieces for years, sometimes decorating the lighthouse. Ultimately, however, virtually every single recovered item was lost, in a rather astonishing run of bad luck that could give nightmares to any antiquarian. A can of accumulated buttons disappeared in a fire. The precious bones may have been deliberately scattered after a superstitious Cullis grew anxious about their presence. Even the so-called ramrods were rejiggered to make lighthouse repairs.

What remained of the wreck submerged in the Mississagi Strait finally received more scrupulous scientific attention in the 20th century than did the dry bones on Manitoulin. Its approximate site marked for a time by the letter "G" in the rocks above, the sunken relic underwent much examination and debate by American and Canadian authorities. One judged that the timbers were too heavy and the surviving metalwork too well forged to have been done in an 18th-century forest, but for many others, these remnants still had the best chance of being the *Griffin*. Amateur enthusiasts and professional archaeologists and divers have scoured the site and the waters off western Manitoulin for further proof, coming up with ancient bits of metal and nails. But those could have come from any number of ancient wrecks and calamities. There seemed nothing that would conclusively prove the ship's identity. La Salle's original brass cannon, for example, would be the most beautifully metaphorical "smoking gun."

Russell Island was another possible *Griffin* wreck site; there a commercial fisherman named Orrie Vail found forty feet of the remains of a keel and charred hull, at the obscure site on the Bruce Peninsula of Manitoulin, north of the community of Tobermory. As with the other hulk, the wreck had long been public knowledge; but, in his retirement, Vail called attention to it as the genuine *Griffin* (complete with ancestor stories he had accumulated from local Indians that their people had ambushed the ship, killed the crew, and burned the ship). This wreck had a number of champions, including Canadian artist and historian Rowley Murphy, as being the genuine *Griffin*, and a number of books and exhibits proceeded to name it as such, to the point the that the resting site of the timbers became known as Griffon Cove. Despite this, a number of authorities came to disagree, and, in 1978, two years after Orrie Vail's death, exhaustive excavations of the Griffon Cove resident concluded, at least so far as the Canadian government was concerned, that this was not La Salle's ship – but rather a fairly commonplace mid-19th-century fishing boat, whose no-frills construction out of white oak (lacking even a deck) led its confusion with a barquentine of more ancient vintage.

Other reported "*Griffin*" wrecks were announced or alleged near Drummond Island, a few in the vicinity of Green Bay, near Saginaw and on the Detroit River. Quite possibly related to the Luc Dane mythology – or not – were tales of giant-sized skeletons (sometimes more than one) found in caves and burial mounds at South Bass Island in the Lake Erie Islands and in-shore Conneaut, Ohio.

What is the probability that a substantial portion the *Griffin* still survives the centuries, awaiting recovery? Unless she were indeed burned to ashes or scavenged to matchsticks, the chances are surprisingly good. From 1996 to 1997, researchers in the Gulf of Mexico worked to recover remains of *La Belle* – La Salle's river-going ship from his ultimately fatal Mississippi River explorations. The boat had rested for three centuries at the bottom of Matagorda Bay.

A 2007 article in the *Chicago Tribune* listed the *Griffin* at the top of the five most sought-after "lost ships" still undiscovered somewhere in the Great Lakes. Some of the others, including the *Bannockburn* and the *Marquette & Bessemer No. 2*, we shall encounter later (see Chapter 5). Or, more precisely, not encounter. Even as this book went to print, an expedition by the French government's Department of Underwater Archaeological Research was undertaking a submarine excavation in northern Lake Michigan, at Poverty Island, following up on the 2001 discovery of a small, blackened slab of hand-hewn timber. Sonar painted a picture of an object about 40 feet long and 18 feet wide, lodged under several feet of sediment on the bottom. Years of legal negotiations between the archaeologists and the state of Michigan had to be resolved before digging could begin, with the understanding that France had rightful legal jurisdiction – should the object indeed be La Salle's lost property. But nothing was found.

In her vanishing act, the *Griffin* also established traditions that had already been classic folklore of the open ocean, the supernatural notions of forces at work beyond the material world. Some accounts claim the during her construction she suffered a jinx – that the ship had incurred a curse cast by Metiomek, a prophet of the Iroqois tribe, converted to Christianity by the Jesuits. La Salle's relationships with the powerful Jesuit Order of missionaries were prickly at best, and he defied the Society of Jesus by favoring the rival Franciscans and other missionary sects as partners in his personal dealings. Metiomek's "curse," even if apocryphal, reflected the thorny barbs of relationships and enmities into which the explorer-entrepreneur walked, among the Indians and the whites.

A poetic piece of folklore claimed that as the *Griffin* disappeared, a loud drumbeat could be heard, and the mystical toll of the "Ottawa drum" would later echo over the waters when any Great Lakes ship met with similar disaster that left no trace, though this belief does not seem to have persisted beyond the age of sail. (One storyteller has helpfully explained that one must be a true lake-dweller, preferably a full-blooded Ottawa Indian, to be able to hear the Ottawa Drum.) Another yarn declares that Lake Solitude, near Oscoda, Michigan, just north of Saginaw Bay, was once connected to Lake Huron by passage deep enough for canoes and other small craft. When the *Griffin* sank nearby, according to local tradition, the ghostly force of the tragedy somehow cut off the route, turning the passage into a small creek and guaranteeing Lake Solitude its privacy.

It is a long-standing maritime pattern that when a ship disappears with no satisfactory explanation, popular gossip sometimes provides an epilogue: the vessel has become a "ghost ship," a literal phantom who sails beyond her death, visible to onlookers, but ever elusive, slipping in and out of view either on the anniversary of her loss or as a supernatural omen of danger. So it is with the *Griffin*. Sightings of the phantom bark are more ancient rumor than anything that cites eyewitnesses or circumstances. We are only told that Indian tribes who frequented the shore areas of Lakes Michigan, Huron, and Erie saw the pioneering ship with the distinctive profile, as did sailors in the northern end of Lake Michigan. Figures are discerned on board. Writer Todd Clements states that a good opportunity to watch for the phantom is on foggy mornings, on Mackinac Island, looking out from the coast facing the Mackinac Bridge.

The procession of Great Lakes disasters that began with the Griffin is commemorated at the Great Lakes Shipwreck Museum, now stands on Whitefish Point, at Sault St. Marie in upper Michigan. *Photo by Chris Winters, courtesy the Great Lakes Shipwreck Historical Society.*

The ghost of the *Griffin* dematerializes every time one attempts to approach her – so they say. It does serve as a metaphor most apt. In similar fashion, many a wreck-hunter has beheld and studied ancient timbers, or chased down rumors and reports of such relics along the Great Lakes, and conjectured that these may indeed by *the* remains, the mortal bones of the oldest substantial shipwreck tragedy on these mighty waters. But with closer examination the theories dissolve; the hulk turns out to be something more ordinary, and the *Griffin* slips away again, into the mists of time. The first great ship on the Inland Seas. The first great shipwreck on the Great Lakes.

The Battle of Lake Erie, as depicted in oils by Charles L. Cassady Sr., a prominent Cleveland, Ohio, doctor and a painter of wildlife subjects and scenics. *Courtesy Charles Cassady Sr.*

What We Talk About When We Talk About Oliver Hazard Perry

In Which a Perhaps Misguided and Certainly Mis-Timed War Determines the Character of the Young United States of America. Certain Treats of the Life of Oliver Hazard Perry, a Hero for All Ages. Military Disasters and Folly Set the Stage for an Immortal Battle on Lake Erie. Self-Interest, Honor, and Possibly Dastardly Scheming During and After the Combat. Perry's Generosity and Manners Remembered to the End, Even by Vanquished Foes.

In the modern tourist Mecca of Las Vegas, countless strollers have beheld an action tableau enacted outside the giant Treasure Island casino-hotel complex, a crowd-pleasing playlet performed with full-scale ships in pools, costumes, and pyrotechnics. In the sketch, two sailing ships engage in battle. One is a rascally pirate corsair, the other a British man-o-war. At first the pirate vessel sustains heavy damage from the British and their snobbish, comically stiff and bewigged officers. But the pirate captain rallies and fires back, scoring a lucky hit that sinks the Englishmen. The crowd applauds – for everyone adores an underdog.

In another era, long before Treasure Island or even the founding of Las Vegas, genuine war could also be a spectator sport. It was said that the aristocratic classes could (terrain and conditions permitting) go with their servants and their refreshments and spyglasses, take seats upon high ground and watch and dine in comfort and luxury as armies clashed in the distance.

The year 1812 would seem to be an especially auspicious season for mankind's favorite recreation. In Europe, Napoleon's conquests extended into Spain and, most fatefully, into Russia. Denmark's alliance with France lead to battles against adjacent Britain as well as Sweden.

And in the young United States, occupying the eastern portion of the North American continent, ongoing tensions and hostility between the former colony and its parent nation, the British Isles, re-ignited into a shooting war.

The English were still firmly an imperial military and naval presence due to their cities, outposts, and fortifications in what would later be known as the Dominion of Canada. While the British Empire's ongoing battles against Napoleon made the resumption of aggression with the United States an unpopular idea, the Royal Navy persisted in harassing American shipping (often with the forced "impressment" of US sailors into the Royal service). A briar patch of trade embargoes against Britain, against France, snagging their assorted allies and foes, stunted the economy of the struggling United States. President James Madison desired free commerce with anyone at all possible. When an American frigate named *President* fought with the British ship *Little Belt*, the path to open war blazed, spurred on by hotheads in Congress.

A haughty British officer boards an American ship and browbeats sailors – the putative reason for the American War of 1812 – in one of the few Hollywood depictions of the conflict, 1952's *Mutiny*.

Naval warfare, dramatized in a 19th-century British engraving.

If later wars would ring with stirring slogans exhorting patriots to remember the *Maine*, avenge the *Lusitania*, remember Pearl Harbor, the rallying-cry for the War of 1812 was more prosaic: "Free trade and sailors' rights!"

The opinion of historians now is that the war need not have happened at all, at least not the way that it did – and poor international communication was partially to blame. Britain's ongoing concern was the Napoleonic crisis in Europe; the comparatively trivial matter of shipping interference and seizure against the Americans was up for debate in Parliament and very likely the British would curtail the objectionable policies on their own accord.

Other historians consider the War of 1812 practically fated, as a second War for Independence, or a continuation of the unresolved grudges of the first one. A violent sequel that settled America's status as a world power and a united people at last. On the opposite side, according to this version, a number of influential British military men judged a clash against the Americans a likely easy victory – one that would buttress morale and faith in the invincibility of the Royal Navy and discourage a minor epidemic of discontented seamen of His Majesty deserting to American ships.

War on England was requested by President Madison on June 1, 1812, and officially declared by America's Congress (a close vote) on June 18, 1812.

Only two days earlier, across the ocean, Parliament had repealed the hated orders behind the disruption of United States shipping.

Throughout the rest of the world, America's War of 1812 is little remembered – compared to Napoleon's retreat from Moscow that same year, commemorated in epics by Tolstoy and Tchaikovsky. Even in the 21st century, an elaborate comedy video posted on the World Wide Web depicts an American soldier, amidst the musket-fire and redcoats, loudly announcing he has no idea what this war is all about. There isn't even any decent War of 1812 entry on Wikipedia, he complains.

But for the United States, despite the cheerful ignorance of the computer-age generation, "Madison's War" remains unique. When the fighting began in earnest, armies of the British throne advanced upon Chicago (then called Fort Dearborn), New Orleans, and even entered the Chesapeake Bay inlet to incinerate parts of Washington.

If our aristocrats in their elite seats could select which battle to enjoy, the Chesapeake Bay campaign would be considered a premium event. In the Baltimore stage of this engagement on land and sea, during the bombardment of Fort McHenry, onlooker Francis Scott Key was inspired to pen "The Star Spangled Banner," a stirringly poetic description of mortar fire and rockets glaring red in the night (though set to the melody of a pre-existing drinking song about jovialities of the gods of Olympus). It is, thus, to the War of 1812, a mistaken war, an unnecessary war, an ill-remembered war, that the United States owes its National Anthem.

And, unless one counts World War II confrontations against the Japanese in Alaskan and Hawai'ian territorial possessions – or the most hyperbole-ridden views of the terrorist attacks of September 11, 2001 – the War of 1812 remains the one time and the only time that foreign armies invaded American soil.

And American waters. The Great Lakes were a significant battleground. Control of the Great Lakes was vital to victory. Across them the British strongholds in Canada stood fast, with prominent British forts providing headquarters from which to launch attacks and resupply divisions. In the Great Lakes region, Indian tribes allied to Britain also beleaguered the United States troops and settlements. And it was a consequence, if not a secret American motivation for the war, that seized Indian and Canadian land would be a valuable prize.

Yet, as a military force, the United States Navy was poorly equipped for the conflict. The Americans had fewer than twenty warships worthy of the term. Napoleon's ally Denmark, with a fleet estimated at five times that size, had just gone down to defeat against King George. That Britannia ruled the waves was no boastful song lyric; His Majesty's Navy had dealt Napoleon himself a mighty blow in the epic sea battle at Trafalgar in 1805; this victory made the British not merely a European power – but a world power, wherever seaways existed to carry their vessels. Britain would dominate the oceans for the next 100 years or so.

As the War of 1812 began, in terms of sheer numbers, most of the ships fighting for the Americans were privateers. Most infamously, Louisiana pirate brothers Jean and Pierre Lafitte bartered with Madison's envoy, Andrew Jackson, for a government pardon for past offenses, if they and their fight-hardened corsairs and freebooters came to Washington's aid in the Battle of New Orleans, a duty the pirates performed with distinction. Though he was an outlaw nearly all his life, Jean Lafitte is honored with public parks and monuments around the Mississippi Delta.

But on the Great Lakes another nautical hero is synonymous with the War of 1812, has left his name commemorated on maps, bronze monuments, street signs, high-school names, a luxury Toledo hotel and sundry landmarks, and has contributed to the very lexicon of war. Oliver Hazard Perry.

"From the beginning his mother noticed that the boy had no fear of anything," wrote biographer Edwin P. Hoyt, which would seem to be the judgment of public opinion and posterity. Historian Gerard Altoff says that, as a military strategist, Oliver Hazard Perry showed no extraordinary genius, but rather a pattern of charging boldly, even recklessly, into situations where another leader might have hesitated or exercised caution. Moreover, at variance with the many statues and paintings idealizing a man of heroic dimensions, Oliver was not very physically imposing, but somewhat short and stoutish and chronically susceptible to illness – a fact that would ultimately prove his undoing. Yet he would become more famous than presidents, and his victories still stand in the annals of the United States Navy as mythic and singular.

Serving on the water must have truly been in the blood of the Perry family. Descended from Edward Perry, an immigrant from Devonshire, they included eight naval officers, and, as biographer Hoyt pointed out, two daughters who married naval officers. Further back, Gerard Altoff writes, the Perry lineage can be traced to none other than William Wallace, the much-mythologized Scottish rebel-hero of *Braveheart* renown.

Oliver Hazard Perry's father was Christopher Raymond Perry, a lieutenant who fought the British during the American War for Independence – not only off the Atlantic coast but also the British shores. Christopher Perry took part in an equally valiant and foolhardy effort to sail an armed brigantine clear to England and lash out against King George III's ships in their own territorial waters. Not surprisingly, he and the crew were captured, Perry sent to prison camp in Ireland, from which he escaped after eighteen months. He managed to make his way back to American soil in 1783, just after the end of the war.

Working as a merchant seaman on the Atlantic, Christopher Perry met and married Sarah Wallace Alexander – who he met at sea, when she was a passenger – and they settled to raise their family on a Rhode Island farm. There, Oliver Hazard Perry was born to the couple on August 23, 1785.

In 1798, under the second President of the United States, John Adams, the US Navy numbered only six frigates. Congress authorized a program to expand the young nation's sea power, and Capt. Christopher Perry, as a Revolutionary War hero and veteran sailor, offered his expertise. He thus won an appointment as "post-captain" of the Navy. A new warship, the *General Greene*, was built specifically for his command. Young Oliver had shown an innate interest in navigation and seamanship and wrote to his father asking to be a midshipman aboard the *General Greene*, an appointment the youth received in 1799.

Perry biographer Edwin Hoyt mentions an incident that gives some indication of the fiber than ran through father to son. As the *General Greene* escorted a merchant vessel through the Caribbean, a British man o'war, bearing seventy-four guns, hove near, intending to board the American merchantman for a forced inspection. The out-matched *General Greene* nonetheless fired a warning shot, apparently to the amusement of the British captain, who wondered why he could not come aboard. The quote from Capt. Christopher Perry: "If she were a first-rate ship with her 120 guns she should not do so to the honor of my flag."

Christopher Perry retired not long afterward. In 1802, Oliver Hazard Perry was transferred to the *Adams*, a 28-gun warship on which he was soon appointed acting lieutenant. The warship went across the Atlantic to assist in the first international crisis to seriously test American strength, the banditry of the notorious Barbary pirates. On board the *Adams* and later the *Constellation*, the *Nautilus*, and the *Constitution*, Lt. Perry saw action at Tripoli and rose in esteem as a well-liked young officer of 22.

Back in the United States, he was put in charge of a flotilla that patrolled the eastern seaboard, principally to prevent unauthorized dealings between rogue American ships and the increasingly imperious British. In 1810, Perry's name made the newspapers of the era as a naval hero. Commanding a vessel named *Revenge* with a small fleet of three gunboats off the coast of Georgia, he retrieved a disputed ship from the British, defying the superior speed and firepower of the sloop-of-war HMS *Goree*. It was more of a matter of brinksmanship – and the prudence of the British captain of the *Goree*, judging that the matter was not worth violence, letting the Americans and their hotheaded commander have their way. But nonetheless, the image of Perry standing firm on the waves against a mightier enemy would prove prophetic within just three years.

The end of the *Revenge* was not in the fog of war but in the more conventional variety. Enveloped in thick January fogbank, she wrecked on rocks off Connecticut in 1811, Perry seeing the entire crew to safety before he was last to exit the sinking ship. The court-martial inquiry into the loss of the *Revenge* (Perry not faulted) and respite from active service allowed Oliver Hazard Perry a hiatus to return to his home on Rhode Island, recuperate – and marry Elizabeth Mason, 20, daughter of a Newport doctor.

When war with Britain finally erupted in 1812, Oliver Hazard Perry's initial duty was to patrol the presumably threatened northern Atlantic coast now with a dozen gunboats under his command, in a still-unimpressive US Navy. Perry seemed to feel it a waste of his talents. But the Great Lakes, though farther from England's ports, proved to be a more crucial battleground.

Whosoever controlled the Great Lakes could well determine success or failure in the entire conflict, and Washington, D.C.'s overall strategy had been some time in the planning. First an army would march from Dayton, Ohio, to Fort Detroit and proceed to smash British fortifications on western Lake Erie, especially Fort Malden and the Amherstburg Navy Yard on the Detroit River. From New York state, the Americans would take the mighty British installations and settlements on the Niagara River. A third force would cross the St. Lawrence River and conquer Montreal.

Had all those actions succeeded, there is a strong chance much of what is now eastern Canada would now be the United States. But the optimistically considered attacks all failed disastrously.

The Great Black Swamp, a nearly impassible region south and east of Detroit, foiled the offensive from Dayton – one soldier who tried to get through its quagmire wrote home that it was the "home of Satan." Ultimately, without reinforcements, the American general at Detroit had to surrender to a small number of British without a struggle. The New York crusade fought some bloody battles at Queenston Heights but halted when local militiamen, expected to support the Army regulars, decided they wanted no part of crossing the river against the British once serious shooting started. The incursion into Quebec, with New York and Vermont militiamen, similarly deteriorated into squabbling between the more- and less-committed American factions camped around the north end of Lake Champlain. At one point in the confusion, one American force wound up opening fire on another.

The British struck next. A small group captured Mackinac Island, between Lake Huron and Lake Michigan, and found themselves encumbered with more American prisoners than they could properly manage. A number had to be released by the British under a "cartel" agreement, a sort of honor system that the POWs would not engage straightaway in resistance against the British (many did, nonetheless). Twice the British sallied from Amherstburg and attempted to take the Americans' Fort Meigs on the Maumee River. One especially alarming tactic were cannonballs heated to a red-hot state before being fired into the fortress, in hopes they would happen to ignite gunpowder arsenals within. The spent, hissing orbs literally boiled the ground on which they landed, a disconcerting sight. But, despite many casualties and a determined siege, the defenders and massive walls of Fort Meigs held. Days after the arrival of 1,200 reinforcements from Kentucky on May 5, the British withdrew (we will encounter these Kentuckians again later).

The British and Indian allies again tried to take the fort in July, but that siege was far less intense than the first and ended with nearly no American casualties. Fort Meigs still stands today and is a landmark historic site in Perrysburg. American defenders on the Sandusky River also repulsed the redcoats, who pulled back to Fort Malden.

There was no question, despite the stalemate on land, that the British controlled these inland seas, with six formidable warships. The only US fighting vessel of consequence had been taken with the fall of Detroit. Daniel Dobbins, an American ship-builder/captain – and one of the refugees from the Mackinac debacle – had a personal audience with President Madison informing him of the humiliations on western Lake Erie. After a cabinet meeting, President Madison decided to build a fresh navy of four gunboats for the fighting on the lake, the construction overseen by Captain Dobbins. In the end, Dobbins and shipwrights, after some confusion, disputes, and second-guessing with the Navy department's Commodore Isaac Chauncey, built six ships at Presque Isle, near Erie, Pennsylvania. The first one whose keel was laid was named the *Niagara*.

The United States' sea forces, though severely lagging in numbers of vessels and men, still could put up a fight. Several significant ocean victories early in the war even had the London press asking: "What is wrong with British seapower?" It was apparent that the young American nation had a population of excellent shipbuilders. The hasty constructions at Presque Isle on the Great Lakes, wrote historian and novelist C.S. Forester, were all the more remarkable for having to labor in haste and improvisation, under a chronic shortage of material. Wooden pegs substituted for the standard iron nails. To pass with ease over the shallows of Lake Erie in particular, Dobbins oversaw "shallow draft" designs. These schooners could sit higher in the water and, in theory, go where heavier British battle cruisers could not. But they risked tipping over during abrupt actions, or even from the recoil of their own artillery.

"Carronade" cannon arrays set up inside a warship, in a 19th-century British engraving.

Meanwhile, Oliver Hazard Perry was dissatisfied with his routine patrol duties on the Atlantic. When he learned of an entirely new fleet forming on the Great Lakes he sent a letter of interest. It was answered by Commodore Chauncey, who knew Perry and gratefully accepted the 27-year-old Master Commandant. In February 1813, Perry received his orders to report for duty to Sackets Harbor, on Lake Ontario.

Given the plethora of landmarks, statues, and namesakes that were to accrete to Oliver Hazard Perry, one might assume the young officer universally well-liked. This is untrue, and historians have since tended to portray Commodore Chauncey as one of Perry's numerous nemeses. Perhaps the most even-handed viewpoint is that the American strategy for a Great Lakes offense, like so much of the War of 1812, or the US naval force itself, was not very well coordinated or planned, and inevitably fractured into vested interests. Chauncey wanted Perry's services – but as an underling.

Chauncey himself planned to command in decisive action against the British, and he would rather have had the American warships built at his own stronghold. For this reason, Daniel Dobbins' Presque Isle shipwright-works and naval HQ found itself routinely starved for men and material that was instead hoarded at Commodore Chauncey's Sackets Harbor.

The choice of Presque Isle on Lake Erie had been Dobbins', based on its outer barrier of sand bars that the heavy British warships could not cross (and that communications to and from Washington, D.C. were slightly more convenient). But it remained vulnerable. British patrols could – and did – keep watch on a blockade from a distance, and there were spies among the Americans. At several intervals, the British forces chiefly massed at Long Point on the north shore of Lake Erie and might have attacked and crushed the growing threat, but misunderstandings, overconfident carelessness, false assumptions about the state of Presque Isle's defense – and perhaps a sense of chivalry now completely lacking in modern warfare – kept the enemy forces distant, maintaining a blockade while the Americans sought to ready for battle.

During this wait, Perry joined with Chauncey on Lake Ontario for an attack on Queenstown and other British settlements on the Niagara River. This time the Americans prevailed, gaining control of a vital waterway, and the Presque Isle station was rewarded with a small number of captured light gunships to add to its fleet. But what Oliver Hazard Perry desperately needed were trained sailors to operate a growing flotilla. Instead Chauncey detained the best of the manpower at Sackets Harbor – includingd more than 100 hand-picked warriors Perry had brought from Rhode Island. Only the least fit arrived at Presque Isle. Perry combed surrounding communities for recruits, but found virtually nobody qualified. In frustration, he sent angry letters to the Secretary of the Navy complaining of Chauncey's intransigence, a breach of chain-of-command etiquette, not to mention respect.

Meanwhile, the key warships in the Presque Isle force, the *Niagara* and the *Lawrence*, were completed. Commodore Chauncey's unhelpful hand here is recorded by historians. From Sackets Harbor Chauncey had ordered heavier cannon installed on the brigantines. This modification weighted them down to the point that when they tried to leave their harbor at the beginning of August, they grounded on the protective sand bars that Dobbins had foreseen as deterring the British. For agonizing days Perry and his crewmen labored to remove all cannon and other weight and maneuver the ships free. They were quite literally sitting ducks for the more powerful British blockade ships under Commander Robert Heriot Barclay.

But Barclay's fleet was largely absent during this crisis – and when they did appear and saw the stripped-down brigantines... Barclay turned back for Long Point. There are rather curious alibis given for this blunder: Barclay was summoned to an important banquet, or that he mistakenly perceived the Americans as having him outgunned (instead of being thoroughly disarmed!) with the wind in their favor. Why Commander Barclay did not press an attack on a growing enemy fleet during its bumbled embarkation remains a minor mystery of the conflict.

Even with his ships off the bar, Perry still had an inadequate amount of men. Bit by bit, he had accumulated more sailors throughout the spring and summer of 1813, including a small group of marines. But the numbers were still insubstantial, and such was his resentment against Commodore Chauncey that before setting out on his campaign against the British, Perry sent another letter to Washington, D.C. – offering to be relieved of command.

He embarked before there was any chance of a response, however, much in the manner of those Americans who had voted for war before there was time to learn that Britain had ended its policy of bullying US ships. And, in fact, Lieutenant Jesse Duncan Elliott, a liaison between Chauncey and Dobbins, arrived at this late stage from Sackets Harbor to join Perry, bringing more than a hundred additional men, including officers. Elliott was given command of the *Niagara*, apparently on Chauncey's orders. And these were orders that Perry did not dispute – at least at the time.

Elliott's career had intersected with Perry's at a few fateful points. J.D. Elliott had also fought against the Barbary pirates. Afterwards he had been assigned to the frigate *Chesapeake*. In 1807, off the coast of Norfolk, Virginia, the *Chesapeake*, with Elliott aboard, was the victim of an act typical of the unseemly British tactics of the era. The formidably armed HMS *Leopard*, at full battle stations, drew aside the Americans and demanded to search for alleged deserters. When the American Captain James Barron refused to be boarded, the British raked the unprepared *Chesapeake* with devastating cannon fire. The damage, dead, and wounded multiplying, Captain Barron was able to only loose one shot as token resistance before surrendering, an act which cost him his career. The ignoble defeat inflamed much American anger, including Oliver Hazard Perry's, and it is possible war may have been declared at that early stage, had not President Thomas Jefferson resisted.

When the hostilities began in 1812, J.D. Elliott made a minor name for himself in guerilla-style raids launched from Buffalo, boldly capturing weapons and small boats to add to the miniscule American naval force. In the meantime, his old ship, the dishonored *Chesapeake*, under Captain James Lawrence, was formally challenged to a sea duel off New England by Captain Philip Broke and the HMS *Shannon*. This time the contest was more even; both ships were armed frigates, each carrying thirty-eight cannons. Broke's gunners were lethal, however, besting the *Chesapeake* within fifteen minutes by savage bombardment. Captain Lawrence was mortally wounded, in agony from a musket ball in his groin. But on the deck he spoke orders not to surrender, even if the ship had to be sunk. His words appeared in different variations and paraphrasings, but they gave the lexicon what would become the most famous quotation in naval combat: "Don't give up the ship!"

Oliver Hazard Perry had been friends with Lawrence, and he had "DONT GIVE UP THE SHIP" stitched into a flag he flew from the mast of his own ship when she set forth with his fleet on Lake Erie on August 12, 1813. Commodore Perry's ship, furthermore, was named the *Lawrence*, in tribute to the fallen officer.

With the *Lawrence* and Elliott's *Niagara* as the most heavily armed dreadnoughts, the American fighting expedition on Lake Erie sallied with eight additional smaller gunships and 400 men spread between them – many of those men ill with an influenza outbreak that, briefly, would afflict Perry himself in the coming days (for lack of viable sailors one sloop had to be left behind altogether at Presque Isle). The ships, though not as heavily outfitted with long-range weapons as the British, outnumbered the six of Barclay's British fleet, and this was an important propaganda point. One immediate objective of the sortie was to gather Fort Meigs' commander, General William Henry Harrison, and twenty-six Indian elders at the Lake Erie islands. Tribal leaders came aboard the *Lawrence* to behold the cannons firing and see for themselves that the British were not the only force capable of bringing "big canoes" to the lake. It was a warning for the natives not to join the uprising of the great chief Tecumseh, who had allied his confederation of tribes with the British against American settlers.

From the south shore of Lake Erie the fleet received 130 more soldiers, courtesy of General William Henry Harrison's army. They were largely marksmen from Kentucky, those Fort Meigs reinforcements, who proved themselves surprisingly adept on the water. Then it became a matter of waiting for the right opportunity to engage Commander Robert Heriot Barclay's full force, especially Barclay's flagship, the *Detroit*. By Perry's reckoning, she outclassed anything he could muster.

For nearly a month Perry's fleet made its base at South Bass Island, off Sandusky and Port Clinton in western Lake Erie. The American boats patrolled in search of Barclay's vessels, and their presence had an effect, in the meantime, as a show of force that discouraged the vital British supply lines to the forts beyond Detroit. Meanwhile, Daniel Dobbins, so instrumental in building the Great Lakes fleet, missed the approaching battle; he had sailed back to Erie aboard the schooner *Ohio* for supplies. Some think that under different political circumstance Capt. Dobbins might well have commanded the fleet he had done so much to raise.

There remained the matter of the illness which had felled so many of the troops. Cool drinking water was a recommended treatment, but even the depths of Lake Erie presented only tepidly warm refreshment. At the last minute, Perry and his scouts found a large limestone cave – one of many on Middle Bass Island – and replenished their supplies with cool water. To this day, the location is known as Perry's Cave.

Just as the gunfight at the O.K. Corral, so well remembered, was in truth finished only in a matter of seconds, so did the Battle of Lake Erie only last a matter of some three hours. It happened on September 10, 1813, a day that dawned clear with favorable wind and weather for both sides. In the young daylight, a lookout announced that the sails of the British fleet could be seen approaching, emerged at last from their lair at Amherstberg.

Perry set out from the Lake Erie Islands to meet Barclay's fleet, with the *Lawrence* and the *Niagara* designated as the chief warships to lock horns with the *Detroit* and the *Queen Charlotte*. Commodore Perry had worked out an entire diagram of engagement in advance, ship by ship. As Perry observed that the *Detroit* was not sailing precisely in the formation he had anticipated, he revised his battle plans (simply shouted by officers to other ships), putting the *Lawrence* in a prominent position against the *Detroit*, J.D. Elliott in the *Niagara* trailing behind. This change may, in retrospect, have led Capt. Elliott to make a fateful, unilateral decision.

Though the prevailing winds gave the American fleet an advantage at the outset, it was unsteady, and Perry saw his fleet beginning to fall out of formation as the British neared. At about 11:45 a.m., there was no more time for second-guessing. The British, as per tradition, had musicians on board the flagship, the *Detroit*, and these men now sounded the anthem "Rule Britannia" as a stirring prelude to opening fire. The first shot from Barclay's guns plopped harmlessly in the water, but the second struck the *Lawrence* firmly, causing the first deaths. The Battle of Lake Erie had begun.

The *Detroit*'s long-range guns pounded the *Lawrence*, and the ship could only take the punishment for a torturous half-hour, as Perry sought to draw near enough so that his own weapons could unleash a carronade. In the meantime, cannonballs, grapeshot, and shrapnel-like splinters of wood from the blasted *Lawrence* maimed and killed numerous crewmen.

Perry might have been a quick casualty himself, but for one uncharacteristic action. Oliver, who would so proudly uphold military tradition on other occasions, instead this day went into battle "dressed down," attired like many of the common sailors rather than sporting a conspicuous gleaming uniform singling him out like a bull's-eye target. Still, the luck that Commodore Perry had that day was unbelievable, as he incurred no injury while more and more of his men fell around him, bloodied and gruesomely dismembered.

Despite supporting fire from the scattered small sloops of the Americans into the firm British line, the mauling of the *Lawrence* grew worse. Perry's battle plan had called for the *Niagara* to stay in formation and primarily fight the *Detroit*'s deadly consort, the *Queen Charlotte*. But the *Niagara* was simply not there! She had gradually lagged behind during the approach, as far as two miles, and now, idled out of cannon range even for Barclay's longest guns. With no opponent, the *Queen Charlotte* joined the *Detroit* in blasting Perry's ship.

Capt. Elliott's reasons for hanging back have been discussed ever since. In the most generous possible interpretation, he may have been confused by Commodore Perry's last-minute alteration of the battle schematics; seeking to maintain his position relative to the other ships, as Perry had ordered, left him away from the thick of the action. That is, again, the most generous possible interpretation.

Or could Elliott have lost his nerve? This may have been so, though it is worth remembering that he performed with valor in leading small-scale raiding-parties earlier.

The cruelest explanation handed down to us by some historians is practically out of the Old Testament – reminiscent of 2 Samuel Chapter 11, in fact, in which King David disposes of an inconvenient romantic rival in his own ranks, the warrior Uriah the Hittite, by sending him to the front lines, then secretly ordering the army's commander to fall back, leaving Uriah to be overwhelmed and slain. Applied to 1813, this theory claims that J.D. Elliott, older by a few years than Oliver Hazard Perry, coveted command of the entire American Great Lakes fleet. Cunningly edging away from the fight, he foresaw exactly what the British would do – pour everything they had into the *Lawrence*. This would probably kill Perry, an outcome that would promote Elliott to commodore.

So, for whatever reason, Elliott's *Niagara* stayed aloof from the battle for an excruciating two hours, during which the crew of the *Lawrence* fought back as best they could, but suffered agonizing losses. A blood-slathered sickbay in the *Lawrence*'s wardrooms, under surgeon Usher Parsons, tried to cope with a steady stream of the maimed and the dying, while Commodore Perry himself would appear at times to summon up onto the gundecks any man in condition to fight. Usher Parsons started out with six assistant medics; eventually he had none.

Through loss of men and mounting damage, the battered *Lawrence* was left by 2:30 p.m. with no more working cannons. The smaller American sloops did harass the British line with their guns, one of them firing a long-range shell that tore though both the captain and the first mate of the *Queen Charlotte*, making the two key officers gory corpses on the deck. But still the British concentrated on the *Lawrence*. Now the American flagship was essentially helpless.

In the mythology of the popular science-fiction drama *Star Trek*, there is a battle-simulation exercise called the "*Kobayashi Maru*," a test of determination for every aspiring Starfleet captain. In it, the cadet takes the helm of a starship rendered defenseless by an alien attack. With enemy ships relentlessly closing in, what does the captain do?

The "*Kobayashi Maru*" does not have a solution; for *Star Trek*'s fictioneers, it is more a psychological evaluation of character in the face of inevitable defeat. Yet the future's James Tiberius Kirk, through guile, beat the "*Kobayashi Maru*."

And, in a similar situation, on planet Earth on September 10, 1813, Oliver Hazard Perry did, too.

As the *Lawrence* lost her ability to fight, the untouched *Niagara* belatedly drew close. Commodore Perry decided to lower his flags – but instead of surrendering, prepared to transfer them, symbolic of his command, to the other warship.

Nothing in the rules of naval engagement forbade such a transfer of command; it was just rarely, if ever, done. On a flagship as perforated as the *Lawrence* had been, the chief officer could be expected to be dead or incapacitated, as the *Lawrence*'s own namesake had been left on the *Chesapeake*. And how often had a first-rate, fully armed, virgin warship materialized out of the smoke and flame, waiting to be used? But fate, circumstances or treachery had presented a physically sound Perry with a perfectly untouched attack ship at the ready. As Spock might have said, the course of action was logical.

Tethered to the *Lawrence* was a small cutter deliberately kept on the side of the ship away from the heat of battle; thus it remained as untouched by the British barrage. Perry rounded up a handful of surviving crewmen strong enough to row (including his own younger brother, the ship's purser) and entered the boat with his flag of command, "DONT GIVE UP THE SHIP." When the flags had been lowered, Barclay likely thought that a formal surrender was imminent. Straightaway, as the boat cast off from the shattered *Lawrence* with Perry actually standing upright in it, oarsmen pulling with all their might for the approaching *Niagara*, the British realized what was happening and opened fire anew at the tiny vessel.

One of the ubiquitous bronze statues to Oliver Hazard Perry and the Battle of Lake Erie, here in Cleveland, has one of the more accurate visions of the legendary "Transfer of Command" (inset). *Photos courtesy Lucy McKernan.*

Perry's transfer of command would become a favorite subject of artists of naval battles, who depicted a gallant Perry erect in the longboat, standing in ornate, full uniform en route to the other ship amidst an inferno of artillery. Except for the costuming (Perry had the DONT GIVE UP THE SHIP banner wrapped around his shoulders), this seems more or less accurate, with the others in the boat beseeching the Commodore to lay low, as cannon, grapeshot, and rifle fire whizzed passed. Remarkably, unbelievably, no harm came to him. Had

Perry indeed been killed at this point, historians might never have agreed on the wisdom of his actions.

The boat reached the *Niagara*. If Capt. Elliott had indeed hatched what amounted to a murder plot against Perry, it was moot by now, and biographers claim he welcomed the Commodore aboard with a few words of politeness, rather absurdly under the circumstances. He offered no Isaac Chauncey-like resistance when Commodore Perry immediately took charge of the vessel; moreover Elliott, on his own initiative, boarded the cutter to inspect the other American sloops. This act may or may not have put him further out of danger. It certainly did remove him from Oliver Hazard Perry's sight.

A strong wind, practically out of a Hollywood epic, now billowed the *Niagara*'s sails and drove her to the enemy line. That same breeze proved catastrophic for the lead British ships. Commander Barclay would also later report that a rudder malfunctioned, although that could have been battle damage suffered later. For whatever reason, the *Detroit* and the *Queen Charlotte* angled too close to each other. The bowsprit of the *Queen Charlotte* fouled through the rigging of the third mast, or mizzen, of the *Detroit*, and the upper riggings of the ships brushed each other and entangled. The flagships of the British fleet were locked together now, incapable of steering.

The *Niagara*, still taking fire, opened up with a broadside on the immobilized ships that had been the Royal Navy's best hopes for victory. Still, as she passed close enough for a simple pistol-shot to fly lethally between ships, the British let loose volleys that killed or wounded twenty of the *Niagara*'s crew. But the Americans had broken through the line of Britsh ships, not just with the *Niagara*, but the variously armed sloops of the Presque Isle navy – *Scorpion*, *Ariel*, *Caledonia*, *Tigress*, *Porcupine*, and *Trippe*. These smaller ships harassed their opponents as well as inflicting further torment upon the *Detroit* and *Queen Charlotte*.

In the final minutes of the battle, the Royal Navy's sailors, through frantic hacking away at ropes and sails, did manage to free their two flagships from mutual entanglement, but at the cost of their own maneuverability, the *Detroit* having been particularly savaged by American fire and most of her guns out of action. Her Commander, Robert Barclay, had himself been wounded twice, a bullet in his remaining good arm retiring him to his quarters even before his ship had locked with the *Queen Charlotte*. His replacement junior officer, Lieutanant George Inglis, saw that the battle was lost and gave the order to surrender.

One by one, the British ships struck their flags – all but two lightly armed sloops that tried to dash west to warn the fort at Detroit. Commodore Perry ordered the *Scorpion* and *Trippe* to pursue, and the two fugitives were also persuaded to yield.

The casualty figures of the Battle of Lake Erie are accounted on the American side as 27 killed, 96 wounded, though there may have been more than a dozen extra dead, out of what Gerard Altoff estimates as 568 combatants spread through the American fleet. Barclay would report 41 killed and 96 wounded out of a total fighting force of 560. It is said that when the British offered their swords in surrender, Perry allowed them to keep the ceremonial weapons, saying they had been bravely worn. This gesture would not be forgotten.

If Capt. James Lawrence had given the world the phrase "Don't Give Up the Ship," the words that Oliver Hazard Perry dispatched from shore, written on the back of an envelope to General Harrison, became the second most quoted in naval conflict: "We have met the enemy and they are ours; two ships, two brigs, one schooner and one sloop." A victory over the British would have been remarkable. But the capture of their entire fleet? Momentous, and still unparalleled in the annals of the United States Navy.

Many dramatists and writers have sought, as in Remarque's novel *All Quiet on the Western Front*, to demolish the thought of war as any kind of noble profession. But in his treatment of the troops under Barclay's command Commodore Perry seemed to exemplify the best in soldiering. He apologized for not having more than one surgeon available to attend to all the British wounded (one of the chief surgeons was still stick with fever), of whom Barclay was one. For a few days, Perry worked with Barclay's representative, Captain O'Keefe, over details of the surrender, while the shattered *Lawrence*, whose decks had seen so much blood, became a floating hospital – fortunately, she was still seaworthy, if only just that.

After two days, Perry met officially with Barclay in his sickbed to compare their actions undertaken under fire, without rancor, as two military gentleman of high rank with reports to serve to their respective superiors.

Here Barclay revealed that the American gunfire had cut down not only the leadership of the *Queen Charlotte*, but had cost the *Detroit* three of her best officers early in the battle, creating disarray amidst the crew. Other British ships had seen similar challenges, as American gunfire, credited often to the Kentucky marksmen, eliminated the most experienced seamen. The rest of the foe were, as with the haphazard Presque Isle navy, many green conscripts from the surrounding Canadian provinces, with little sea legs or nerve for fighting.

Indeed, just as supplies and men had been scanty for the Americans, so they were for the British. Nineteen frightful cannons of the *Detroit* had been scavenged from an inland fort and installed on Barclay's flagship when the intended artillery did not reach Detroit from a British base on Lake Superior. Not designed for marine use, the land weapons presented a hardship to load and fire – and they were of six different types, requiring the *Detroit*'s harried gunners to scramble through a confused supply-arsenal of six incompatible varieties of shell.

Both men came away with respect for each other, and Perry offered to pay for Barclay's expenses in returning to England.

The electrifying news that the confrontation had been won by the Americans spread throughout the young nation and made Oliver Hazard Perry as famous as Presidents Jefferson and Madison. In Philadelphia, a massive commemoration over the Battle of Lake Erie was accounted the largest public celebration that city had yet seen. At age 29, Oliver Hazard Perry became the most popular man in the nation.

But another officer would not share that view. By September 11, the American fleet and captured British ships were all moored at Put-In Bay, while Perry composed his official report to the Secretary of the Navy. It is for modern historians to read a little between the lines here, in light of subsequent events, and a lengthy feud one commentator has come to call the "Second Battle of Lake Erie."

In his account, Perry commended the performance of J.D. Elliott aboard the Niagara, minimizing Elliott's late arrival into the battle. This might have been, by modern standards, a phenomenon that would recur in American military history down through the ages – an official whitewash. The battle was won, and Elliott had an influential family and supporters. In ironic modern vernacular, perhaps Perry saw no point in making waves.

Elliott himself read Perry's words and approved them – at first. Then he began to entreat Perry to further de-emphasize the fact that the *Niagara* remained out of the initial fighting. It is reported Perry conferred with a trusted fleetmate on the matter who thought Elliott was getting far too much credit already. So Perry let the matter drop – for the time being.

There was still a war on. Perry joined the armies of William Henry Harrison and a fresh influx of a thousand mounted American soldiers to attack the British at Detroit. In fact, the easy defeat of Detroit by the British was now inverted; the British General Henry Procter, after the victory at the Battle of Lake Erie, pulled inland in more or less full retreat. What resistance the pursuing armies did encounter came from Great Britain's allies, the Indian warriors who had rallied around Tecumseh's confederation. Oliver Hazard Perry followed the enemies' withdrawal as far up the Thames River as he could in shallow-draft sloops, then left the boats under the command of Elliott, while Perry went to meet Procter's forces where they had finally turned to make a stand.

History – or at least legend – records a stirring image of the battle of Thames River at the settlement of Moraviantown (now in present-day Ontario, near Thamesville). Oliver Hazard Perry was on horseback, rallying troops in the front of the battle lines in the style of a naval officer – not in the rear with the other land generals, planning strategies in the safety of their tents.

The American side had been heavily fortified with Harrison's Kentucky riflemen thirsty for revenge for the defeats in the early stages of the war. The British-Indian alliance was overwhelmed and defeated. Tecumseh, whom William Henry Harrison would call one of the great generals of the ages, died in battle. Tecumseh's prediction that the white man's government in Washington, D.C. would soon seize Indian land as spoils would sadly come true.

Except for British holdouts on Mackinac Island, the War of 1812 in the northwest corner of America was now over, and Perry requested a transfer for himself, as well as safe passage for Robert Barclay and his men. When the mingled fleets arrived at Erie, Pennsylvania, putative home port of the Presque Isle ships, the community held a torch-lit parade in Perry's honor. Perry quieted the crowds so Robert Barclay, quartered nearby, could sleep and recuperate in peace.

Before leaving, Barclay would make a gift of his navigational sextant to Oliver Hazard Perry and later, back among his British countrymen, toast the young Commodore as a "gallant and generous enemy."

It was the end of Perry's career on the Great Lakes. Though the Americans held the north-central arenas and had vanquished the Indian-British alliance, the war raged, and the Navy Department approved Perry's request for a transfer (ironically, sent in frustration before the victory of the Battle of Lake Erie) closer to his home in Newport and the Atlantic theater of battle. Perry did receive a hero's welcome and was obliged to sit for portraits and appear at grand balls. But there was no letup in the fighting. Here, where a massive Royal Navy, not just a small token fleet, patrolled with close to impunity in the open ocean, cities suffered. Perry was in charge of countering the powerful enemy and repelling the scattered British land incursions. It was in July and August, 1814, that British might struck most boldly, ground troops under General Robert Ross marching through Maryland and Virginia, defeating the American's land forces and burning buildings of the Capital in Washington.

Perhaps it is to the credit of the British that this calamity is so little remembered by the present generation of Americans. Under a strong code of warrior honor, the targets were military, administrative, and infrastructure, designed to weaken the American resolve; atrocities, pillaging, looting and raping, and tormenting civilians were not, in this particular case, accepted as proper martial behavior. Hungry British troops did help themselves to very fine meals in the White House before setting fire to it.

Perry rushed to the Potomac River, near Alexandria, to inflict as much damage as possible on British warships. In an instance strikingly reminiscent of Horatius at the bridge, he is said to have found, with the help of local residents, a large 18-pound cannon that had not seen action since the Revolutionary War. Nonetheless, it was the only sizable gun available, and with this lone weapon Perry bottled up and bombarded a convoy attempting to leave the Potomac, ceasing only when cannonballs ran out. All the while the British ships fired at their single antagonist. Perry and his squad suffered no casualties.

From there, Perry hastened to assist in the defense of Baltimore, a key city the British had expected to take with relative ease. For Perry, the matter was keenly personal; a warship specifically for his command, the *Java*, was under construction there. But the lessons of Washington had been learned, and when the enemy attacked Baltimore in September, the defenders at Fort McHenry were ready. Although Royal Navy cannons pounded the shores for nearly forty hours, unleashing a state-of-the-art weapon – the rocket – troops could not establish a footing on land. A separate British ground assault led by General Ross, coming from the southeasterly direction of the ruined Washington, met a determined force of militia and riflemen.

Two of the Americans, mere youths not destined to live beyond the battle themselves, opened fire on an officer on a distinctive white horse. Thus, they killed General Ross, whose death demoralized the land army, though the British pressed on. After days of stalemate with the American resistance, however, remaining British officers conferred and decided to withdraw.

Perry had remained awake for forty-eight hours straight during the battle. He was anticipating the completion of the *Java* and taking the ship into action, but before that could happen, the British had sent by messenger the Treaty of Ghent. Although American victories on the Great Lakes, at Baltimore, and the later Battle of New Orleans gave a popular impression of America's having "won" the War of 1812, the truth was that, in April of 1814, Napoleon Bonaparte had been defeated on the other side of the Atlantic, rendering most trade issues and alliances with France and its allies no longer an issue.

Continuation of the war on American shores at all was – and largely had been – purely punitive. The British Empire did not seriously expect to re-take their former colonies, just demonstrate to them what lay in store for nations who challenged His Majesty. Indeed, when Washington, D.C. fell, partially in ashes, there were some voices raised on the British side that things had gone a bit too far.

The United States economy itself had been wrung dry by the war (so had the embattled Britain's), and many American politicians were working behind the scenes to finally end it by negotiation. The cessation of hostilities was signed formally on Christmas Eve, 1814. Later historians would try to put things in proportion by calculating that, for the United States, the War of 1812 has cost only a tenth as much damage and loss as the Civil War (and that estimate seems modest). Author Harry Coles called its resolution a "peace without victory," and, putting it flatly, wrote "nobody won."

Certainly the Indians lost.

Oliver Hazard Perry's victory appears in comics, centuries apart. First, a snide American political cartoon from 1813 shows the King and Queen of England upset at the news…

…And a 1942 American propaganda comic-book story imagines ghosts of the Battle of Lake Erie *still* fighting from their respective sunken wrecks – until paranormal troubleshooter "Sgt. Spook" reconciles them with the update that America and Britain are now united against the Axis.

Yet, according to C.S. Forester, the valiant American performance, especially on the water, had earned valuable British respect and, in some odd way, solidified the future longstanding peacetime and wartime friendship between the USA and the United Kingdom. It might be noteworthy that Forester (creator of iconic naval hero Admiral Horatio Hornblower) was a British transplant to America who worked assiduously to cement strategic alliances between the English and the Americans, in two World Wars. Actually, throughout the mid-1800s, as Washington, D.C. and the British Crown competed in continental expansion, many Americans continued to suspect British malice, particularly behind the hostile Indians tribes opposing further white settlement out west in what became the Blackhawk Wars.

In 1842, when the writer Charles Dickens toured the Great Lakes area via steamship, he read in a Cleveland newspaper bellicose calls for Britain to be "whipped again" in yet another war, one which would culminate in triumphant soldiers of the Stars and Stripes singing "Yankee Doodle" and "Hail Columbia" in a conquered London. For that, and for other breaches of etiquette, Dickens refused to meet the mayor of Cleveland or any inhabitants of that city, and he stewed aboard the steamer *Constitution* until she departed for the next port, Buffalo.

Certainly key participants in the War of 1812, like General William Henry Harrison – a US president, albeit only for a matter of months before dying of illness in 1841 – would find themselves parlaying their palpable patriotism into public office and honors later in the century. But Oliver Hazard Perry would not, it turned out, be among them.

There was, first, the unfinished business of J.D. Elliott and the "Second Battle of Lake Erie." Although he had been honored equally as Perry with medals and commemorations and a share of prize money, the other officer still nursed a smoldering obsession that his handling of the *Niagara* had been perceived as insufficient, even disloyal. After the war, Elliott repeatedly sought to restore his reputation. He solicited British veterans from that day to confirm he had fought in the thick of the battle. One is on record as saying instead that in the Royal Navy conduct such as Elliott's would have led to a hanging. Elliott charged that Perry, according to the rules of engagement, should have been considered a prisoner of the British since the *Lawrence* had technically lowered her colors and surrendered from a distance – although she had not been boarded by the foe and formally taken captive. In the spring of 1815, Elliott staged a public "inquiry" in New York Harbor in which his handpicked assortment of witnesses and officials further affirmed that Elliott's opportunity to join in the fighting was stymied because the British seemed bent on avoiding the *Niagara*, not the other way around.

The verdict held no particular legal import except as anti-Perry propaganda. However, Perry was having troubles of his own, those that tend to make one reflect that if luck had been with the young commodore throughout the War of 1812, it seemed to desert him later.

His great frigate *Java* completed her final fittings in February, 1815, just in time for President Madison's ending the war that many thought was so unnecessary. Nonetheless, a revitalized United States Navy, now with combat-tested men, still had jobs to do. Pirates and North African potentates in the Mediterranean had taken advantage of America's distraction with the British to continue their mischief, and, in 1816, Perry took the *Java* across the Atlantic with three other ships, all commanded by War of 1812 heroes, all under Commodore Isaac Chauncey, to enforce treaties and intimidate the chronic threat. On this mission – besides discovering too late that the *Java* had inferior construction courtesy of a shifty contractor – Captain Perry came to be at odds with another foe within his own ranks, a marine captain aboard the *Java* named John Heath.

As with J.D. Elliott, John Heath finds few champions among later historians, though his conflict with Perry might have been one of personality and style – the classic "odd couple," but with military honor involved, not just personal taste and hygiene. While Perry comported himself as an officer, spit-shined and representing to the world the finest of the United States in manner, education, and bearing, Heath did not set himself particularly above any of the other marines under his watch (an aspect that probably endeared him to them). He was said to be informal in dress and habit, if not downright sloppy, overweight and lax in discipline.

One of more obscure conspiracy theories of American history proposes that John Heath secretly worked as an agent for J.D. Elliott, somehow actualizing Elliott's will to undermine Perry all the way across an ocean, at the *Java*'s anchorage off Tunisia, without benefit of long-distance communications. Such a remarkable feat of collusion is unlikely. But in any case, Heath and Perry clashed bitterly. At one point Captain Perry, fed up with Heath's insolence and the demeanor of his marines – and perhaps under the influence of alcohol served at a feast that night – struck the other man across the face during an argument.

Although Perry lost little time in setting down a formal apology on paper, a court martial ensued for this breach of conduct between two officers. Immediate consequences seemed minimal, as both were called into Commodore Chauncey's quarters for a reprimand, then sent back to duty. The matter required the sequence of events be entered into the record, which did indeed list the infractions and disrespect shown by Heath and his men. But when the *Java* returned to the United States, Heath would not let the matter drop. Newspapers, particularly in the marine Captain's native territory of Virginia, took up Heath's side against the northerner Perry. There was only one resolution, apparently – a formal duel.

Dueling in those days was not uncommon as a means for "gentlemen," in and out of military service, to ultimately resolve a personal feud or vendetta. One such duel had claimed the life of founding father Alexander Hamilton, shot dead on a New Jersey shore by Aaron Burr. In the New Orleans area particularly, dueling had become a popular, deadly pastime; many fencing schools thrived on teaching aspiring duelists the art of the swordfight. We are told that young sports in the Louisiana metropolis, with the assistance of alcohol, would often duel purely for the thrill, many falling gravely injured or dead as a result. When pistols – especially new models that testified to the high quality of the American gunsmiths' craft – came into vogue as dueling weapons the fatalities rose sharply.

After the issuing of challenges via their go-betweens, Oliver Hazard Perry agreed to a duel of honor with John Heath on October 19, 1817. Though the initial dueling ground was preferred to be Washington, the match was instead held on the very same patch of New Jersey field overlooking the Atlantic where Alexander Hamilton had fallen. Heath and Perry stood back-to-back, then walked away from each other the traditional five paces and turned. Heath was to fire first and he did. His shot missed.

Oliver Hazard Perry's rightful turn came next, but he did not aim and fire. Instead, his companion, Stephen Decatur, read aloud a letter Perry had written to him many months earlier, outlining a plan for the duel. In the message Perry admitted his fault in raising his hand against Heath, a fellow commissioned officer, and as atonement, should he meet his foe on the dueling-field, Perry would refrain from shooting.

Heath declared himself satisfied with this – as well he might have been, escaping a likely death. And so was that feud settled. There remained, however, J.D. Elliott. He continued to write letters, to Perry and others, charging that Elliott's credit for victory on Lake Erie had been stolen by Perry. When Perry, the Heath affair behind him, could take no more of this, he sent a letter to Elliott holding nothing back about the other officer's "disgraceful conduct" in battle.

J.D. Elliott, perhaps unsurprisingly, had been a duelist himself on previous occasions, and now he challenged Perry to a contest of arms to decide who was right. Perry refused – thus conveying the message that while Heath had a legitimate cause for his grievance and deserved an apology, Elliott merited nothing of the sort.

Furthermore Perry broke a long professional silence by sending the Secretary of the Navy a note detailing in full Elliott's maladroit and suspicious performance at the helm of the *Niagara* as the *Lawrence* suffered. But Washington (now under the administration of President James Monroe), for whatever reason, had no desire to resurrect the ghosts of the Battle of Lake Erie, and no inquiry or court martial took place regarding Elliott's demeanor and actions five years earlier.

If J.D. Elliott had any closure in his bitterness against Oliver Hazard Perry, it was that he would outlive the other man by a considerable span. In 1819, the Navy asked Perry to lead a fleet of warships and sloops to South America and partially up the Orinoco River, a bit of saber-rattling to demonstrate to the government of Venezuela, then in rebellion against the empire of Spain, that American merchant ships were not to be targeted by opportunistic pirates and privateers loosely affiliated with the Venezuelan freedom-fighters.

The United States' ships carried heavy guns. But throughout Perry's career, no artillery could avail against perhaps the deadliest enemies of all, disease microbes. Fever and illness had befallen Perry and his shipmates before in their voyages, even on the eve of the Battle of Lake Erie. Now a fever outbreak was rampant in the sweltering tropics around the Orinoco. In letters back to Washington, Perry warned of men dying all around him, the infection spreading to his ships and his in-shore lodgings. Nonetheless, requirements of diplomacy kept the American hero in the midst of the epidemic. His presence was requested particularly for a grand banquet of August 14, the night before Venezuelans dedicated their new constitution.

As soon as he possibly could, on August 15, Perry embarked on the Orinoco toward the open sea where the frigate *John Adams* waited to take the Americans home. But by the time his schooner reached the mouth of the river, Perry began to display all the worst symptoms of deadly yellow fever. Soon he was prostrate aboard the *John Adams*, the ship itself becalmed and its sails hanging limply. By August 24, with the ship still motionless, Perry realized he was dying. He dictated his will, leaving everything to his wife, and, at 3 p.m., he died. He had just turned 34.

That mosquitoes transmitted the virus that caused yellow fever was unknown at the time, and – for fear of possible contagion spreading – the dead were often buried where they succumbed. Taking Perry's body back to his home and family in Rhode Island was, thus, not an option. Accompanied by a ceremonial firing of cannon, the corpse was brought ashore on the island of Trinidad with full honors provided by the Third West India Regiment.

Know, reader, that the Third West India Regiment was a British regiment, for Trinidad was a possession of the Crown. Yet it welcomed the fallen hero who had captured an entire fleet of His Majesty's on Lake Erie. It is written (and one would especially like to think it true) that among the soldiers in the West India Regiment were a quantity of veterans from Robert Barclay's freshwater navy – the selfsame men whom Commodore Perry had allowed to retain their swords after the defeat, because of "the bravery with which they had been worn." Now these men were able to show their respect in return, and they raised funds for the governor of Trinidad to erect a monument over Perry's grave.

Already, ships on the Great Lakes were being named in Commodore Perry's honor. A first written biography arrived in 1821. In 1826, an American sloop-of-war – under the command of Capt. Daniel Dobbins – arrived at Trinidad and took Perry's remains at last back to his home and family in Newport, under another granite monument. The Lake Erie Islands and Put-In Bay would eventually see reunions of veterans of the Battle of Lake Erie, and, finally, in 1913, the dedication of the Perry Victory Memorial, a tall Doric column with a figure of the Commodore atop it, a view that could easily see across the inland sea to Canada. In recognition of the enduring friendship between the United States and Canada, one of the longest undefended borders in the world, it bears the title of International Peace Memorial.

Jesse Duncan Elliott was promoted to a captain in the United States Navy in 1818 and commanded various ships over the ensuing twenty-seven years, though the shadows over him continued when he was charged with misconduct in 1840 and suspended from duty. Not long after resuming his captaincy, he died in December, 1845. Unless a quorum of historians come forth with a version of events that revises his image, he seems fated to remain forever a villain of the piece, the Salieri to Perry's Mozart in a grand opera of battle.

One may at least propose that if not for Elliott's course of action – or inaction – on September 10, 1813, the warship *Niagara* would not have served in pristine condition. After the victory, she worked as a "station ship" at the port city of Erie. At the conclusion of her duty, she was scuttled at a place called Misery Bay, a not-uncommon method of retiring wooden ships into "storage," sometimes temporary, sometimes permanent. Mercifully, as the 100th anniversary of the

Battle of Lake Erie approached in 1913, area citizens followed through with an audacious scheme, to honor the occasion by raising the decayed hulk from the depths and floating her again.

This was done, and the exhumed *Niagara*, handsomely restored, participated in the Centennial at Put-In Bay in September, 1913. On that occasion she was towed to the ceremonies. In 1931, the state of Pennsylvania undertook a long-term project (made even longer by the Great Depression and the second World War) to more fully rehabilitate the *Niagara*. It took until 1943 to complete work on her hull, and 20 years more to fully outfit her masts and riggings with her more than 12,000 square feet of canvas sail. In the late 1980s, a further restoration, timed to the 175th anniversary of the battle, ended with the brig beautifully outfitted and seaworthy again, relaunched on September 10, 1988. Based out of Erie, she has participated in numerous "tall ship" gatherings around the Great Lakes and along the Eastern Seaboard, representing Pennsylvania's maritime heritage.

The gloriously restored brig *Niagara* under sail. *Photo courtesy Caleb Pifer.*

The Perry family itself contributed more men to the young United States Navy. Of Oliver's brothers, one became a lieutenant, another a midshipman, another a purser – and another a commodore, one whose name also attained celebrity, albeit in such a context worlds away from Oliver Hazard Perry. Few seem aware the two men are related.

Matthew Calbraith Perry, said to be more reserved and thoughtful than the outgoing Oliver, followed his own War of 1812 service in the Atlantic with four decades of duty at the behest of Washington in various world trouble-spots. He worked to modernize the United States Navy, pushing for the abolition of the practice of flogging as punishment. He spurred the introduction of steam-engine power to supplant the old riggings and sails that left fleets at the mercies of the winds. And he brought artists adept in life-painting – and later, early photographers – on board his ships, to record historic scenes for posterity as they truly were. One wonders if those outsized, heroic renditions of Oliver rowing to the *Niagara* under fire played a part in Matthew's desire for accuracy.

Matthew Perry's fame endures especially for a feat achieved late in his life, the 1852 "opening" of the closed empire of Japan. With America in an expansionist mood in the Pacific (Perry worried particularly about countering Czarist Russia), this Commodore Perry boldly steamed into Eddo (Tokyo) Bay, commanding a group of four warships – fewer than he had requested from President Millard Fillmore, and underpowered in the worst-case-scenario of a fight. But, impressing the Japanese with canny combinations of flattery, unsubtle displays of American weaponry, his own firm confidence, and generous gifts of technology and know-how (including an entire miniature locomotive and the collected works of Audubon), Matthew Perry negotiated the 1854 Treaty of Kanagawa. It established formal relations and alliances between the two countries and cultures eras apart.

And, less than a century later, when the modernized and emboldened Japanese Empire went to war against the United States in the Pacific, the United States Navy that responded was composed of many officers who had graduated from the United States Naval Academy in Annapolis – a school Matthew Perry had helped bring into being.

There have been those who suggest, especially in light of his brother's varied and successful career, that Oliver Hazard was one of those men of action who could only come into his own in a crisis, when he could plan tactics or execute strategy. When not at war, it seemed, he fell into doldrums of petty squabbles, routine assignments and, perhaps, drinking too much. Such a conclusion would certainly satisfy those moralists who sought rhyme and reason in Oliver's almost tragicomic death, far away from the fray, in a colonial backwater because he had to stay for a party; it was as if a changed world had no more use for him, just as the great Lawrence of Arabia would perish in a silly motorcycle accident. But this viewpoint does a disservice – "sophistry," Gerard Altoff calls it. Nobody knows what Oliver Hazard Perry might have achieved had he survived the malarial tropics.

At Annapolis, there can be seen to this day a heroic mural depicting the *Niagara* under the command of Oliver Hazard Perry, as she finally enters the field of fire during the Battle of Lake Erie.

The bow of the *Success*, featuring the ship's figurehead, later to be stolen. A recreation in watercolor by Great Lakes diver and wreck-hunter Georgann Wachter, who, with her husband Michael, has written and illustrated several books on the hulks that lie beneath Lake Erie. *Courtesy of Georgann Wachter.*

The *Success*
The Ship That Lived for Shame

In Which a Merchant Barkentine of Noble and Sturdy Construction Somewhat Arbitrarily Becomes Symbolic of Evil. Treats of the Early Australian Settlement and the Fateful Role Played (or Rather, Not Played) by the Aforementioned Vessel. Ignominy and Hatred, Violence and Murder, Profiteering and Nostalgia. Tales of Torture and Ghosts. The Notorious Success *Remains Seaworthy Whereupon the Mighty* Titanic *did not. A Watery Lake Erie Repose at Last Under Suspicious Circumstances.*

The end came on the night of July 4, 1946, with a denouement that could be seen from the southern shores of Lake Erie along the beaches of Sandusky and the resort town of Port Clinton, Ohio. It was the end for one of the most infamous sailing vessels in history, a ship that – in the minds of many – was the most vile thing to float.

Her history was unparalleled. With the possible exception of folklore's *Flying Dutchman* and the unfairly-besmirched mutiny vessel HMS *Bounty*, not since the earliest known records of men on boats, the South Sea Islanders, the Greeks and Phoenicians, the outriggers, the Indian canoes, the pirogues and the rafts, was one single ship so widely reviled, and systematically maintained as a tangible symbol of man's terrifying inhumanity to man. That it even existed at all, in the 20th century, it owed only to showmanship – an uneven mix of entrepreneurial greed, historical appreciation, and morbid fascination, that this was *the* ship of horrors. These planks witnessed where the crimes were committed; these walls heard the screams when the damned were punished.

Halfway around the world there were now places becoming widely known, places with names like Auschwitz, Bergen-Belsen, Treblinka, and Dachau. Landlocked, these hellish prisons would also be preserved with great care, their shadows intended to fall on succeeding generations as a symbol of absolute evil. But their careers as museums of malignancy had scarcely begun. This ship had already carried her dark burden beyond a human lifespan. And, like the Wandering Jew of myth, the ship shouldered her weight of sin from continent to continent, circumnavigating the planet, and ever would so until...Judgment Day, perhaps?

In fact, it was Independence Day, 1946, the first such that the United States had enjoyed following the conclusion of a dreadful World War. The first peacetime summer season that the hotels, cottages, marinas, and amusement parks of the Lake Erie Islands and western port cities had known for five years. Ever since the Japanese Empire had rained death from the skies upon more distant islands in the Pacific in 1941, a good portion of America's population had been soldiering abroad or defending on the home front. Now the fighting was over. The boys had come home, to young families, pre-fab houses, fresh inventions like the suburbs and television, and a new era of prosperity, promise, and a thousand uses for plastic.

There was a note of triumph in fireworks all along the cities and towns rimming the vast Great Lake Erie – which, in area, ranks as the twelfth largest natural lake on Earth. But Erie is also the shallowest among the monumental five sisters, Superior, Michigan, Ontario, and Huron. A shallow sea coupled with widely navigated waters means, inevitably, shipwrecks. One in particular, off Port Clinton, had been stuck above the waterline for many months.

As those Roman candles and rockets flew into the warm early-evening air on that July 4, it might at first have seemed like an answering light was coming from the surface of Erie, only about a half-mile out. The weather was good, and many yachts and pleasure craft were drifting idly in the twilight. When the light grew in size and revealed itself to be a fire, a fire on the water, there was a fear that one of the innumerable small vessels had exploded. But the inferno grew, and grew, much too large now to be small craft.

It was *the* ship, on fire, where she had run aground a year earlier. Now some trespasser had set fire to her. She burned below the waterline, until lake waves extinguished the blaze. Reporters had a field day describing how the many trapped souls must have soared, wailing and keening, out of her hold, freed from "Floating Hell" by the cleansing flames, as the old ship died.

Her real name was supremely ironic: *Success*.

She was a 135-foot, 600-ton, three-master fashioned out of sturdy teakwood. The *Success'* oft-published biography claimed that she sailed and served in a monstrous capacity as a member of the "First Fleet" to New South Wales, Australia. This was the forced English colonization of the Antipodes by miserable boatloads of lawbreakers, debtors, prostitutes, rebels, and condemned prisoners expelled from Great Britain in the late 1700s. In wave after wave of prisoner – and supply – transports, ultimately between 150,000 to 165,000 such "settlers" embarked unwillingly from the British Isles.

The British, shortly after the European's discovery and mapping of the Australian coast, had determined that a colonial beachhead in this far-off corner of the globe would be advisable as a countermeasure against the spreading tendrils of rival empires such as France, Holland, and Spain. However, the "First Fleet" carried the added benefit, not far in intent from the infamous "Mariel Boatlift" that disgorged undesirables from Fidel Castro's Cuba in 1980. It was an act of social-engineering by the ruling classes to send their least wanted elements into long-term exile, as far off-planet as one could get.

Australia was not the only such destination for the unlucky and unwanted. Many far-flung British colonies served this ancillary function, and before the troublesome Revolution of Adams, Jefferson, and Washington, about 1,000 former British subjects annually arrived in North America not by choice, but by deportation. The Declaration of Independence in 1776 curtailed using the thirteen colonies across the Atlantic and aggravated prison overcrowding in Britain. Britain's eventual response, the Transportation Act of 1784, ultimately decided on Australia as a new "Place or Places, Part or Parts beyond the seas" to which to dispatch troublemakers.

The initial load of 733 convicts ranged in age from a 9-year-old chimney sweep who had stolen clothing and a gun, to a woman of 82 who had committed perjury (and, after surviving the trip, she hung herself, the new colony's first recorded suicide).

For most, it was a choice between being sent to Australia or face execution by hanging on (or, specifically, above) English soil. For those who opted for exile, the sentence need not necessarily be permanent, but carried a stipulation of seven to fourteen years, assuming the prisoner survived. For lawbreakers more extreme, the pronouncement "for the term of his natural life" became the punitive catchphrase of the length of relocation.

Arthur Phillip was appointed the first governor of the territory christened New South Wales; thus, it also fell to him to oversee the prisoner-transportation problem. He was a retired Royal Navy captain with the added experience of having served in the employ of the Portugese Navy. History looks more or less favorably on Capt. Phillip's part in the First Fleet. A sensible officer, he knew better than some of his bureaucratic contemporaries the logistics in making such a long sea journey, and he fought the apathy and callousness of his colleagues to ensure the ships carried adequate (if just barely) food, water, and provisions. Without his foresight, the situation could have degenerated into true horror.

Still, conditions were overcrowded, sickness rife. Prisoners crouched throughout the journey in deck compartments without portholes, adequate ventilation or lighting, brought up to the deck for exercise under armed supervision – even though there were not even sufficient stores of cartridges for the guards' firearms, in the event a prisoner revolt took place at sea. None did, though one man did briefly escape in an early port and was recaptured. A total of forty-eight people, convicts and crew alike, died of sickness and infirmities en route. A plan to send a few faster ships ahead in advance of the First Fleet, to unload provisions at the destination, came to naught.

Ultimately, the First Fleet numbered eleven sailing ships, departing in May 1787. Six carried the human cargo of convicts, with segregated ships for men and women; and two – the great warship *Sirius* and the small sloop *Supply* – held troops, administrators, and cannon, in case of interference from pirates, hostile aborigines, or other nuisances. They sailed from Great Britain first to the Canary Islands, then Rio de Janeiro (spending a month in port while the *Sirius* underwent caulking and Capt. Phillip renewed old Portugese friendships). From Rio the fleet followed a customary long-distance route that caught the trade winds and currents, back across the Atlantic to South Africa and Cape Town, where the ship spent another month, as Phillip made additional bargains with the Dutch colonists for livestock and other supplies. It would not be until January 18, 1788, 252 days after their initial departure, that he made landfall at New South Wales, two days ahead of the rest of the First Fleet, and more than 15,000 miles from England.

That the *Success* was involved in this harsh exercise would have made her nearly as old as the American Revolution. Popular printed accounts of the notorious ship put 1790 as the date she launched – built in Burma by the British for the East India trade. For a dozen years afterwards she did honorable work, transporting spices, silks, teas, and gems amidst foreign and exotic ports, her decks trodden by great merchant princes and nabobs. It was in 1802, however, that she found her new calling, as one of the regular England-to-Australia prison transports.

Technically, therefore, her reputation as belonging to the "first" First Fleet could not have withstood scrutiny. In fact, the ships of the "Second Fleet" arrived at Australia throughout the month of June, 1790. They were informed of an important change of plan. Phillip had immediately found Botany Bay to be dry and unsuitable for European-style farming (aborigines did subsist the area; they greeted the newcomers with calls of "Warra warra!" literally translated as "go away!"). After only five days, he and his scouts judged a previously unexplored inlet to the north, Port Jackson, to be more hospitable, with lush greenery, an abundance of fresh water, and a harbor worthy of visitations and anchorage by future fleets. This would become known as Sydney Harbor, home to the metropolis of the same name.

The Second Fleet had the distinction of the worst rate of mortality en route; one out of four died in the trip, making exile to Australia a more literal than metaphorical death penalty. And Sydney Harbor was hardly a paradise for the settlers, who suffered famine and crop failures from 1790 to 1792, starvation only averted at one point by the lucky arrival of extra goods from Calcutta, India. The "Third Fleet," with more than 1,800 convicts, many in miserable condition and a ten percent death rate in transit, landed at Sydney in 1791. Following that, it seems, there was no point in numbering the prison-transport shuttles out of England. The Transportation practice continued until 1868.

Now-Governor Arthur Phillip was adamant that the convict relocation be a humane project. He wrote "there can be no slavery in a free land and consequently no slaves." The marines and military officers he oversaw – none of whom had ever intended to make New South Wales their lasting home – were often outraged that Phillip punished their offenses worse than he did the convicts. Nonetheless, prisoners disgorged by the various fleets, especially in the early years of settlement and deprivation, were subject to brutal discipline for the merest infractions and inevitable escapes and mutinies.

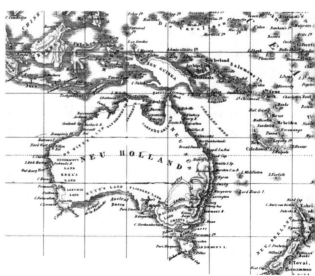

An old Dutch map of Australia – or, as the imperial power preferred to call it, "New Holland."

Later tales of the *Success* revived the grimmest days of early New South Wales in pamphlet form, descriptions of the wretches and rebels whipped until their flesh turned to jelly and the whites of their bones showed; of the rapes and prostitution that occurred on the female convict ships; of the back-breaking toil on the new farms, ranches, mills, and housing that Botany Bay, Parramatta, the Hawkesbury River, Van Dieman's Land, and the hopefully named Liberty Plains would need to become self-sustaining.

All these sins, in hindsight, were engraved by storytellers and moralists into the teak-timber grain of the *Success*. Yet in truth, she did not even exist when most of this took place.

Many respected Great Lakes historians and chroniclers, when they recounted the *Success* story, even into the late 20th century, after her demise off Ohio, accepted without question she was nearly as old as the American Revolution. But no. The ship described as a cruel relic of the Transportation Act was not at all present in the Sydney Harbor settlement. That was later embroidery, by profiteers, once her fate as "Floating Hell" had been established as a commercial proposition.

She was, in truth, built in Moulmein, Burma, of sturdy teakwood – not, however, in 1790. Rather, she launched a half-century later, in 1840, for Cockerell & Co. of Calcutta. The wooden walls of her hull were two feet, six inches thick at the bilge. Her stern was of an old-fashioned "square cut," while her bow, initially unornamented, was fitted after a few years with a demurely clad female figurehead. Her initial career was indeed that of a merchant trader, a three-master built strong enough to withstand long journeys over multiple oceans, from the East Indies to the British Isles, carrying goods and services to the bustling ports of England, the seat of the Empire.

Early in this career, however, she suffered minor grounding on a reef on the way to England. Summarily, Cockerell & Co. sold the *Success* to London merchant Frederick Mangles. This – and not with the Transportation Act – is when the "Floating Hell's" Australian connection began. Mangles determined he could reap more profit by accepting a charter to take settlers to one of the new settlements in rocky, sparsely inhabited western Australia, the other side of the continent from New South Wales.

Swan River was not, initially, a prisoner-relocation endeavor. Rather, it was a capitalistic venture, pushed by an English entrepreneur named Thomas Peel, to turn an obscure outpost into a profitable colony for investors. Much seed money, in fact, came from a convicted thief from an 1814 prison-transport who had served his time out and prospered as a merchant and banker in Sydney. The 1829 boatload of Swan River colonists at the inception were free people – but, sadly, both they and their would-be squire, Peel, found the land not as fertile and easy to tame as first supposed. As a commercial gamble, Swan River failed, though its desperate supporters kept the colony struggling along. It was to this hard-luck place that the *Success* brought its first immigrants, workers to help shore up Swan River's wobbling infrastructure. After the new settlers were landed, however, a small boat carrying the temporary captain of the *Success* capsized; the ship's master drowned with several others. When the *Success* returned to England, Mangles sold her off.

Her next trade journeys under new owners went to Jamaica, India, and

British Guyana. But she had proven herself on the Australian circuit, and she continued to ferry passengers to and fro at ports around the antipodal continent. It is worthy to note an ironic postscript to the Swan River settlement, that, in 1850, the area – now officially the state of Western Australia – finally offered its services to Britain as an additional prison-labor colony, since the further dumping of convicts in New South Wales had fallen into disfavor in some quarters. But the *Success* was not part of this late phase of the Transportation Act.

What sealed the handsome ship's notoriety was the great gold strike in 1851. As white settlements and fortune-seekers penetrated the continent they found rich copper deposits in particular, and gold – that ore most divine to the newcomers – had been sought and small discoveries declared by various individuals. But the California gold rush of 1848 opened the floodgates. An Australian named Edward Hargraves traversed the Pacific Ocean to find his treasure on the North American continent. He returned dissatisfied, with little to show after two years' prospecting in North America, but he determined that the untapped Australian continent held more promise and fewer hardships. Putting his California acumen to work, Hargraves set up gold sluicing and panning works. He named a potential mining-site after the El Dorado-like city of Ophir in the Old Testament, gaining public and press attention. And, like a modern investment-opportunity presenter at the corner Holiday Inn, he gave public presentations on gold-mine operations. Hargraves' genius was that his new goal lay not in making money off the metal laboriously extracted from the dirt – but by having his investments in government licensing and legalities required to service the gold frenzy he ignited. He retired a rich man indeed.

The Australian gold rush, beginning in Ophir, but soon spreading to additional lands in the territories of New South Wales and Victoria and South Australia, brought thousands upon thousands of enthusiastic "diggers," many new to the continent. In the words of a Sydney newspaper, "Mobs are constantly arriving here from Sydney, without food, money, or implements....They evidently came hither with the idea that they could kick the precious metal out of the earth with their heels."

At this time, the *Success* had been in the port of Melbourne, Victoria, in between charters. When gold fever struck the crew, they summarily defected for the promise of riches far more than what they earned as sailors. This identical malady robbed other vessels of their men, and a number of sizable frigates and schooners remained at dock, deserted.

Of the many somewhat surreal concepts in the Australian saga, one that must be recognized is that this state, founded on prison exiles, had to maintain its own prisons. Of course Transportation was not meant to be, as in the science-fiction film *Escape From New York*, an anarchic free-range penitentiary where cutthroats made their own rules. Under the system set down by Governor Phillip, convicts acting as field labor, construction workers, and servants had to be supervised by colonial administrators. After their terms expired, the convicts had the option of leaving the continent or remaining as respectable citizens. And many were pardoned early (though still required to report regularly before the equivalent of a modern parole officer). But in practice, many violators never "reformed," or their behavior grew worse; most indeed had few qualifications or experience suitable to the task of nation-building at all.

In the case of a few notorious incidents in the early days, intransigent convicts (especially Irish ones who had a special sense of solidarity and grievance against the Crown) rose in open revolt and plundering raids. Local military crushed these rebel bands and killed many in open battles.

For such breeds of malefactors, penal settlements such as Castle Hills, Moreton Bay, Norfolk Island, Port Macquarie, and the dreaded Port Arthur came into being. There is a line from the Orson Welles motion-picture thriller *The Lady From Shanghai*, uttered by a worldly sailor, "The best jails are in Australia; the worst are in Spain." But conditions in these Australian prisons-within-a-prison were no lark. Severe whippings would be followed by baths of seawater. Solitary-confinement cells were often filled with water so, should the prisoner sleep, drowning would result. In extreme cases, at Norfolk Island, prisoners would murder other prisoners for the simple reason that their homicide trial would take place at Sydney, giving them a brief vacation from Norfolk Island.

Nonetheless, the inevitable lawbreaker element among fresh immigrants, plus the stampede of new arrivals for the gold fields, meant that, by 1851, the prisons of the prison nation were themselves overfilling with "bushrangers," claim-jumpers, and run-of-the-mill troublemakers. The solution, again lay in the water – not sending these villains to yet another island, but rather, penning them up in disused ships at anchor, which had been an English practice. Five idle ships were purchased by the government of Victoria for this mission and taken to a place called Hobson's Bay, where they clustered as "convict hulks." One of those ships was the *Success*.

Here the *Success* did become a true prison ship. The First Fleet transports, however bad they had been, had not subdivided the cramped living space into cells. That modification was performed on *Success* and her sisters, and the *Success* could accommodate a population of 120, the worst prisoners on the Stygian lower-deck rows. Inmates of this fleet with no destination were brought out of their cells in irons to work at hard labor during the day, forced back aboard at night. Those favored by the guards, considered better behaved or guilty of minor offenses, were accommodated in the larger cells nearer the top deck.

The Norfolk Island prison had been headed by an official named John Giles Price, whose name has a special place in horror among Australians, inspiring at least one memorable villain in the manner of Simon LeGree. He was tall, powerfully built and oddly (for a minor aristocrat of Caribbean birth) able to converse with the captive criminals in their own slang. But his sympathies towards them, if any, rarely encompassed the prison reforms or liberal treatment that was sometimes recommended by the clergy. In crushing a potential mutiny he had overseen a mass-execution (by hanging) of seventeen men in one day.

In 1854, this feared commandant of Norfolk Island was appointed to oversee the incarcerated prisoners of Victoria, an assignment that included the Hobson's Bay fleet. Some of the convicts lodged the ships, the *Success* in particular had earlier been in Norfolk, such as an outlaw named Dan "Mad Dog" Morgan, whose name recognition in Australia remains every bit the equal to Billy the Kid or Al Capone. On March 26, 1857, as Price visited the prison-labor quarries he was attacked and killed by a vengeful, pickaxe-wielding mob of the convicts, said to have been led by Morgan, in a denouement that could have come straight from pages of a storybook.

In 1858, the hardened criminals were moved to quarters on land, and the *Success* saw successive populations of new and different inmates. First were naval deserters, then females and delinquent juvenile males. In 1869, with the Transportation Act finally curtailed, the prison hulks were decommissioned from their morose duty and emptied.

Once again, the harrowing doom-ship history of the *Success* is at variance from facts. Many have written that the Australian citizens despised the outcast fleet at Hobson's Bay and the way of life they represented, and that public anger led the government to sink or break up the hulks, and that the *Success* only escaped dismantling due to a bureaucratic error.

But Richard Norgard, a modern historian who has spent decades researching the *Success* and her cargo of myths, writes that this vengeful act is just not so. Most of the other prison hulks – *President*, *Lysander*, *Sacramento*, and *Deborah* – had deteriorated too far to be of much use, and they duly went to the wreckers. But the sturdy *Success* remained viably seaworthy, and the Victoria government used her for some years as a floating munitions arsenal. Eventually, she was auctioned off to what would become a series of private owners.

In 1890, one of them, a certain Alexander Phillips, belayed his plans to trim the masts and turn the aging ship into a barge. Tales of the Australian bush rogues were rife, such as notorious Ned Kelly, a colorful bandit whose eccentric habit of wearing a badly homemade suit of "armor" to deflect bullets earned him wide fame. Then there was the Charles Dickens novel, *Great Expectations*, built upon the conceit of the dangerous convict Magwitch shipped to Australia and later returning to England anonymously a rich man. Australian penal servitude, or the evidence of it, turned up as clues in the *Sherlock Holmes* tales of Arthur Conan Doyle. Even the ballad that is a virtual national anthem of Australia, "Waltzing Matilda," when heard in its full original "Australian Highwayman's Song," develops into the crime-and-punishment of a swagman (robber) committing suicide rather than being captured.

In 1874, Australian publishers issued Marcus Clarke's *His Natural Life*, a novel (previously a magazine serial) that used the First Fleet convict period as a backdrop for an epic of crime, punishment, and redemption intended on a scale of *Les Miserables* and *The Count of Monte Cristo*. In it, John Giles Price was thinly fictionalized as the sadistic warden "Maurice Frere."

By 1877, after Port Arthur had closed and the celebrations of Australia's centennial had commenced, curious visitors, including celebrities from abroad, took steamships to inspect for themselves the cells of the legendary Australian prison, as well as its successor at Hobart on the Tasmanian peninsula. Everyone wanted to see landmarks mentioned in *His Natural Life*.

Alexander Phillips decided that, with a steady stream of sightseers, a market existed for those morbidly fascinated with the early years of Australian hard-labor settlement a full century ago. And here sat a genuine decommissioned Australian prison ship, complete with cages and a set of corner cells on the lower decks that, with their minuscule dimensions of two feet, eight inches wide, had functioned as "black hole" solitary-confinement chambers.

To that the impresario Phillips and his investors added some enhancements – one might punningly say, excess to the *Success*. These were instruments of torture and torment erected with wax-effigy dummies installed for maximum visual impact. In actuality, many of these tools of cruelty had never been employed on any prison hulk.

There was the whipping-frame, to which prisoners were tied, spread-eagled and upright, for the lash – or conceivably, a branding-iron. There was the "iron straightjacket," a cruel arrangement with a spiked collar and a short chain, designed to keep a convict in a stooping posture. There was "silent guard," a heavy blue-granite stone ring to which twenty convicts could be chained at a time without fear of their being able to get very far. There were the "bilboes," heavy leg-iron cuffs connected by stout rods, limiting convicts to crouching or prone positions. There were chains and manacles of all sorts.

Last, but not least, there was a crude suit of "armor," a doctored bucket for a headpiece, that purported to be the very same protection worn in vain by Ned Kelly when the law finally cut him down. This last, however, was almost certainly a fake. "Genuine" Ned Kelly armor had multiplied across the Australian territories for exhibition, in the same manner that, decades later in the United States, bullet-riddled automobiles would, purporting to be the vehicle in which Bonnie and Clyde perished.

Thus arrayed, and with informative plaques at intervals for the sightseers, the *Success* opened to the public, with Cell 26 shown off as the one in which Dan Morgan himself had sojourned and schemed revenge.

After her opening as a floating chamber of horrors, the *Success* was ready for the big time, a berth for paying customers in bustling Sydney Harbor. From this era we have a story that a veritable lynch mob of local residents, outraged at this dark apparition in teakwood in their midst bringing unwanted memories, stormed the "Original Convict Ship" and sunk her. This allegation is repeated by Australian author, art critic, and historian Robert Hughes in his magisterial best-seller about Australia's colonization, *The Fatal Shore*. But Norgard can neither confirm nor deny it. What is true is that the *Success* sank at Kerosene Bay, Sydney, in 1892, remaining submerged for about six months before being sold off by Phillips and refloated by the new syndicate of owners. It was one of several such accidents during her career – and not especially unusual for any vessel so long in existence. But such are the legends of the *Success* that any such mishap would take on a sinister tone.

From this interval we also have a tale that one day a white-haired old man visited the Original Convict Ship at Sydney. His name was Henry Johnson – alias Harry Power – and he had been an inmate on board the *Success* at Hobson's Bay. An Irish offender (some accounts claim poacher, others claim the theft of a pair of shoes) who had been deported to Australia under the Transportation Act. In the bush, Johnson/Power had turned into something of a "gentleman bandit," and there was a rumor he had mentored young Ned Kelly himself in lawbreaking, before being captured and incarcerated in Cell 24 for seven years. When the management of the Convict Ship learned an actual convict was in their midst, they hired Harry Power to be a high-profile guide on board.

Later, the legend would claim that he held the position for several months, but that the hideous memories of his term on the ship finally overwhelmed him, and he committed suicide by drowning himself into the bay. Less sensational is the more reasonable and better-documented verdict, that the old prisoner-turned-guide tended to drink to excess and took a fatal, inebriated tumble into the water within a year of his being hired. The Harry Power tragedy, favoring the suicide theory, soon became part of the *Success'* promotional yarns, Cell 24 singled out for its role as gawkers filed past.

If making Harry Power relive his past had proven fatal, no such qualms appeared to worry the proprietors of the brigantine when, in 1895, they decided to make the *Success* retrace her way back to Great Britain and tour the port cities with her holdful of horror stories. After some reconditioning and updates, the venerable ship made the journey safely, a testimony to her solid construction. The first British Isles circuit of the *Success* was a sensation, thanks to the very able public-speaking and publicity skills of Joseph C. Harvie, the principle owner-impresario. He also wrote down the first published "history" of the life and crimes of the *Success*, from which many later writers would draw, and further elaborate.

Sailing from one port of call to the next, the "Floating Hell" sold tickets to paying customers throughout the Sceptered Isles for the next fifteen years. Only then did the novelty begin to wear off. For years now, some of the partners in the *Success* had considered taking her across the Atlantic to America. Finally, in 1911, with the aid of an Indiana businessman named David Smith joining the consortium of owners, the decision was made to test the gruesome appeal of the Convict Ship in new waters.

Besides alterations to her sails and structure, there remained one more thing to do before the Floating Hell came to America. Apparently, it was not deemed enough to say that the *Success* saw torture, suicide, and the worst scalawags of an untamed continent. Several decades were falsely appended to the age of the ship; now she was bruited as not merely a prison hulk of the gold-rush era but one of the awful Convict Fleet transports that had made the arduous crossing all the way from England in the opening years of the 1800s, her suffering cargo in shackles. She was not merely damned – but doubly damned.

An astonishing story is told at this juncture, that when the *Success* departed for America, she left the docks shadowed by another vessel, one whose infamy would dwarf even hers – the White Star liner *Titanic*. Crossing the Atlantic Ocean in mid-April, the aged, archaic sailing vessel *Success*, all not-quite-one-hundred-years-old of her, festooned with antique torture-gadgets and crude confinements (though now updated with radio communications), completed the trip more or less without incident. Simultaneously, the 882 ½-foot long, state-of-the-art liner, the summit of Edwardian knowledge and ship-building technology mated with the luxury of plush staterooms, grand staircases, upholstered comfort, a gymnasium – and an on-board orchestra – grazed an iceberg and sank with appalling casualties.

The truth is that the *Titanic* had departed Southhampton five days before the *Success* cast off from a dock near Lancaster on April 15. The *Titanic* had already suffered her fatal hull breech and gone to the ocean floor just as the

Success was getting underway. The *Success* was but one of many boats of varying designs and qualities that accomplished a transatlantic crossing during that same tragic week. But it was to the Convict Ship that the irony stuck fast – even without the showmanship of Joseph C. Harvie, who had retired from association with the vessel in 1908.

The *Success'* initial American travels fulfilled the Convict Ship's name. Of cities on the seashore she visited New York's Coney Island (and, later, Battery Park), Atlantic City, Boston, Newark, Baltimore, Philadelphia, Pensacola, Baton Rouge, and Mobile. The Mississippi River, the Chesapeake Bay, and their network of rivers took her to Washington, D.C., New Orleans, Vicksburg, Memphis, St. Louis, Louisville, Cincinnati, Wheeling, and Pittsburgh. When the United States entered the Great War, on the side of Britain (and Australia), the *Success* did her patriotic duty by serving in Cincinnati and Pittsburgh as a Marine Corps recruitment post.

Nor was she restricted to the Atlantic coast. In 1915, her operators took her through the young Panama Canal to tour destinations on the Pacific shore, including Seattle, Tacoma, Astoria, Portland, and a major engagement in San Francisco's Panama-Pacific International Exposition – the 1915 World's Fair. And the ship, filmed from a passing cruiser, made a cameo appearance in an eighteen-minute travelogue shot at the Fair, starring popular silent-film comics Roscoe "Fatty" Arbuckle and Mabel Normand.

Once in America, the *Success* went Hollywood – in a fashion – by being filmed in *Fatty and Mabel Viewing the World's Fair at San Francisco*, a 1915 Keystone short subject.

It is worth noting a detail mentioned by Great Lakes maritime historian Cris Kohl, that in most of these American exploits, the barkentine was towed by tugboats. The age of steam power, then the age of the diesel engine, had eclipsed the age of sail that had birthed the *Success* so long ago in Burma. After her 1912 transatlantic crossing under a Canadian skipper named John Scott, fewer and fewer active masters or sailors still worked the water who were equipped with the training to handle her.

In 1923, she made her first Great Lakes tour. The Floating Hell would be a regular sight for many harbor towns and destinations on the Great Lakes – Rochester, Oswego, Albany, Kingston, Erie, Sandusky, Cleveland, Toledo, Detroit, Port Huron, South Haven, Benton Harbor, Saginaw, Chicago, Charlevoix, Manistee, Mackinac Island, Sheboygan, Green Bay, Milwaukee. Visits would be accompanied by advertising ballyhoo in the local newspaper:

> She has held lurid horrors and dreadful iniquities beside which even the terrible stories of the Black Hole of Calcutta and the Spanish Inquisition pale into significance...From keel to topmast she cries aloud the greatest lesson the world has ever known in the history of human progress.

A 1924 article may not have been hype when the reporter printed the figure that more than a million visitors had trodden the decks of the "Original Convict Ship."

There were few stunts left untried by the enterprising owners and a succession of hired guides and lecturers to draw attention to the *Success*. Schoolchildren could enter essay contests, carrying a $50 first prize, quite a fortune in those days, for the best-written opinion of the evil ship. Citizens – pretty young girls, especially – tried to set records to see who would last longest in the solitary-confinement cells on a prison diet of bread and water. Couples could be married on board, flaunting various bad-luck superstitions, with black cats, mirror-breaking, and ceremonies in Cell Number 13 as part of the package.

Ghost stories made especially good copy, for what environment that had seen so much unspeakable pain would not be haunted? According to Richard Norgard, the majority of *Success* ghost lore was set down by Harry Von Stack, a twenty-year guide and lecturer on board the *Success* who held a distinctly Manichean view of the battle between good and evil. In addition to the melancholy life history of Harry Power and Cell 24, listeners would hear of ghostly figures seen climbing the riggings. Strange sounds were reported issuing from the hold, and an eerie blue glow illumed the solitary-confinement cells.

Even the fact that a good many of the crew were Russians and Finns – considered reliable sailing-men and cheap to engage – was worked into the mythology of Floating Hell, that as non-English speakers they were ignorant of the *Success'* demonic history and tormented spirits and were the only ones who could be hired on.

Throughout the 1920s and the 1930s, the *Success* weighed anchor – metaphorically; more realistically, tugboats brought her – into such illustrious destinations as the Chicago World's Fair, the Cedar Point amusement park of Ohio, and the Great Lakes Exposition in Cleveland. "THE OLDEST SHIP AFLOAT IN THE WORLD! BUILT IN 1790" read her prominent signage. In fact, those who have followed the news clippings of her history find that towards the terminal phase of her career the Convict Ship drew some interest from Australia, perhaps to retrieve her and convert her into a permanent museum. However, the revelation that she was being brazenly misrepresented as practically First Fleet cooled some of the Australian enthusiasm. It is said the Australians tried to alert Americans that the Convict Ship was not as old as her keepers had advertised, but nobody listened.

The onset of the Great Depression cut into the profits of the *Success*. David Smith left the company syndicate in 1931. A Cleveland proprietor of a printing works become her majority owner, and, after a final tour of the Atlantic coast, the barkentine remained confined to the Great Lakes – for the term of her un-natural life, one might say, as she would never again leave. Except for a few sorties to Michigan, Cleveland became her long-term berth for the latter portion of the 1930s.

By now her reputation as the oldest ship afloat was becoming all too accurate. However, in the years of the Second World War, the old convict hulk drew little interest compared to her earlier circuit. The public consciousness focused on the new nautical innovations in the papers – the submarines, the battleships and the aircraft carriers that were going into combat against the Germans and the Japanese in the Atlantic and Pacific. Crowds gathered for goodwill tours and War Bonds fundraisers by the flying-fortress bomber *Memphis Belle*, not the creaking, leaky, deteriorating Floating Hell.

In the fall of 1942, the *Success* was towed to Sandusky, and in March, 1943, a storm battered her, aggravating her leaks. She sank at her moorings. There a salvage operator named Walter Kolbe acquired the rights to the century-old hulk. By the summer of 1945 he had the *Success* towed to nearby Port Clinton. She drew too deep a draft to enter the shallow Port Clinton harbor, so Kolbe ordered her towed to his property east of the town. There she grounded hard in two and a half fathoms and stuck fast there, despite efforts to dig a trench to ease her closer to shore.

Thus trapped, the Original Convict Ship remained, immobilized and wan, ravaged by Lake Erie storms and a crush of shallow-water ice. There were other indignities as well. One day, an unknown party simply walked out to the ship over the lake ice and sawed off the head of the antique ship's figurehead. Souvenirs from the *Success* still persist in private and public collections all along the lakeshore and in the Lake Erie Islands.

Objects recovered from the *Success* are on frequent
display along the south shore of Lake Erie.

The Coast Guard regarded the derelict hulk as a threat to navigation, and, listing to one side, she certainly presented an eyesore, no matter what her heritage or importance. When she burned on July 4, 1946, there were rumors, quite apart from the wraiths and tortured spirits released from their shackles, that Kolbe himself had set the blaze, tired of the nautical albatross around his neck.

The wreck is still there in Erie's embrace, the tough teak timbers of the hull below the waterline, where the water halted the fire's appetite. What remains of the *Success* is weighted down by a heap of marble for ballast. The devastated relic remains in water easily accessible for snorkel and scuba divers. Few other pleasure boaters and tourists along the Great Lakes resort inlets and marinas here know of the details of this obscure obstruction, that for many years she was indeed the most celebrated – and abhorred – thing afloat.

The proverb goes that success has many fathers, but failure is an orphan. In her century-long career, the *Success* indeed had many fathers, yet in the end was still an orphan.

NOW PLAYING THROUGH JULY 29

Eastland

A NEW MUSICAL

BASED ON THE TRUE CHICAGO STORY

Written by Ensemble Member
ANDREW WHITE

Music by
ANDRE PLUESS and **BEN SUSSMAN**

Directed by
AMANDA DEHNERT

lookingglass
theatre without a net

2011
TONY
AWARD®
RECIPIENT

THE
CHICAGO
COMMUNITY
TRUST
AND AFFILIATES

ART WORKS.
arts.gov

UNITED
Official and Exclusive Airline

Additional support provided by
the STS Foundation

CALL 312-337-0665 OR VISIT LOOKINGGLASSTHEATRE.ORG
LOOKINGGLASS THEATRE ◆ WATER TOWER WATER WORKS ◆ MICHIGAN AVENUE AT PEARSON

The wreck of the *Edmund Fitzgerald* inspired an immortal song – but the calamity of the *Eastland* gave rise to an entire songbook, with the 2012 premiere of this original stage musical done by Chicago's Lookingglass Theatre. *Photo by Sean Williams, courtesy Lookingglass Theatre Company.*

On the Cruelty of Numbers

In which the Worst Ship Disasters on the Great Lakes are Accounted, a Prologue Remarking on the Most Famous – the Edmund Fitzgerald, *Whose Loss of Life Scarcely Begins to Approach the Most Severe Death Tolls. Lake Michigan's Waters Stained by Double Calamities. An Appalling Scene in the Chicago River Goes Strangely Unremembered by the Nation Until Lately. Horrors of Fire and Steam Leave Generations of Puzzled German Tourists.*

Edmund Fitzgerald

At an author event, a fellow attendee told me he had a strange story to tell about the sinking of the *Edmund Fitzgerald*. I thought I had heard most of the strange stories of the *Edmund Fitzgerald*, but this one was new to me. The man's mother-in-law literally blamed herself.

There were no survivors of the 29-man crew when, on the night of November 10, 1975, the 729-foot, 8,686-ton freighter sank on a stormy Lake Superior. She had launched on the Rouge River, south of Detroit, in 1958, the first lakeboat to be built of prefabricated steel subassemblies. Named for the chairman of the Northwestern Mutual Life Insurance Company of Milwaukee, the "*Fitz*" was a truly modern freighter, intended to carry mostly ore and wheat, and she came equipped with all the modern conveniences, two plush passenger staterooms and lifesaving gear. Crew slept not in cramped bunks, but their own individual, comfortable cabins. Dubbed by some "Queen of the Lakes" (by others, probably because of the name, "King of the Lakes"), the freighter's profile became a favorite sight for observing maritime enthusiasts as a flagship of the Columbia Transportation Company. She reliably crossed the waterways, routes taking her from western Superior to Detroit, Cleveland, and Gary, breaking records for cargo tonnage hauled. It is said her crew were so proud, they shooed away gulls from her decks rather than let bird droppings undignify her.

She embarked on what was intended as a final run of her season before winter set in, on November 9, 1975. The "*Fitz*" had been, since 1971, under the command of veteran Great Lakes Captain Ernest "Mac" McSorley. She took a load of iron-ore pellets at Superior, Wisconsin, slated for the blast furnaces of Detroit. A fierce gale and snowstorm blew up, prompting Coast Guard warnings to all vessels on Lake Superior. Captain McSorley consulted by radio with another freighter skipper, Captain Jesse "Bernie" Cooper, of another giant ore-hauler, *Arthur Anderson*. They agreed on a slightly northern route along the Canadian shore, facing the fierce wind.

But the storm was a monster, a cauldron of severe weather extending as far east as New York and as far south as Florida, generating ninety mile-per-hour winds. During a fraught morning and afternoon on November 10, with rough waves pounding both ships, Captain McSorley was in radio contact with Captain Cooper during heavy snow squalls. The *Fitzergerald*'s long-range radar had failed, Cooper stated later, and the freighter was taking on water and listing to one side. At the 3 p.m. hour, the Coast Guard issued an alert for all vessels on Superior to seek safe harbor or drop anchor. There was no such option for the two freighters, persevering in 500 feet of angry water. With Cooper directing the essentially blind *Fitzgerald*, the boats made tortured progress toward the sanctuary of Whitefish Bay.

The "*Fitz*" could barely be discerned visually through the blizzard. McSorley's last words to the *Anderson* on the radio at about 7:12 p.m. were: "We are holding our own." When the snow abated, the *Edmund Fitzgerald* was gone, not only from sight, but from the *Anderson*'s radar as well. Whitefish Bay had only been seventeen miles away.

That was the end of the *Edmund Fitzgerald* and her 29 crewman, with no distress signals sent, no bodies recovered, and only minimal wreckage found. The wreck was later pinpointed 530 feet down, broken in two pieces. The absence of survivors ensured that what ultimately happened to the ship and her men would become a long-term source of speculation.

Had she been dangerously overloaded with iron, to offset the close of shipping season? An inquest decided this was not the case. Perhaps, said some old-timers, the *Fitzgerald* had encountered a wave phenomenon that is virtually mythic, the "Three Sisters." Their exact origin unknown, the Three Sisters are a succession of three large waves that hit in a virtual ship-killing pattern. The first two big waves come quickly, one after another. The third wave lags behind the first two but is much larger, and it delivers the final blow that floods or sinks the boat.

A two-year Coast Guard investigation faulted leaking or unsecured hatches on the decks, aggravated by further dousing down the ship's vents, perhaps ravaged by a log or other piece of lake debris washing about on the deck during the tempest. An inspection in Toledo prior to her final voyage had disclosed some hatch damage, but the defects had been considered within normal safety margins for such a boat.

The Lake Carrier's Association was not satisfied and conducted their own inquest, theorizing the ship had bottomed out on a shoal, a rock formation in the vicinity charted incorrectly by both American and Canadian surveys. Had this catastrophe happened, the disemboweled ship must have filled with water and sank before the crew realized what had happened or had time to send a radio distress signal or reach lifeboats.

But my informant at the book fair had a very different explanation from his mother-in-law. It seems two of the men aboard were her cousins. Before the *Fitzgerald* undertook her ultimate voyage, the pair invited her on board and gave her a personal guided tour of the mighty freighter. She may have been the last person to walk the ship's deck, longer than two football fields, and survive.

Later, after the disaster, she realized that in visiting she had violated an ancient sailor superstition: never have a woman on board – it brings bad luck. Thus whatever did befall the *Fitzgerald* that terrible November night could be traced to her. My source insisted she really believed this, and the guilt and grief tormented her thereafter.

(And it may or may not have brought relief to her to hear, as Sean Ley of the Great Lakes Shipwreck Museum later told me, that the first skipper of the *Edmund Fitzgerald* routinely brought his wife with him on trips, with no commensurate jinx.)

If anything, the story demonstrates the grasp the *Edmund Fitzgerald* tragedy still holds on the lakefront communities. The sinking inspired Canadian balladeer Gordon Lightfoot to write and perform "The Wreck of the *Edmund Fitzgerald*," an evocative song that broke big atypically in disco-dominated pop charts, setting into melancholy folk-melody the dangers of working the Great Lakes, with old Indian legends about Superior in particular, and the oft-repeated refrain:

> The lake so it's said
> Never gives up her dead
> When the gales of November come early.

The music endowed the shipwreck a mystique unlike any other.

The loss of the 29 men is commemorated annually, with bell tollings and the names of the dead read every November 10 at Mariner's Cathedral in Detroit. The area of Superior in which she went down solidified its reputation as the "Graveyard of the Great Lakes." Some claim to have seen the *Edmund Fitzgerald* as a phantom ship.

The bell of the *Edmund Fitzgerald*, on display at the Great Lakes Shipwreck Museum. *Courtesy Paul Wunderle.*

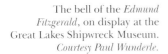

When dive teams (one a Cousteau expedition), robotic submersibles, and documentary filmmakers went down to the wreck and retrieved artifacts, including the 200-pound ship's bell, such were the strong emotions over the *Fitzgerald* that bereaved families of the victims protested angrily to the Canadian government (who had jurisdiction over the territory) at the violation of what they consider a gravesite. In the summer of 1995, when the 200-pound ship's bell was recovered, a replica bell was left behind in the depths as a replacement, with the names of all the crew engraved, for no human eyes to read. Further deep-water expeditions were curtailed.

Yet, in terms of statistics of human fatalities, the Great Lakes, the Five Sisters of Erie, Huron, Ontario, Superior, and Michigan, have taken away lives in numbers far in excess of those 29 lost with the *Fitzgerald*.

In one 20-year period alone, from 1878 to 1897, a calculated 1,166 individuals died in 5,999 Great Lakes shipwrecks. One single great storm on November 13, 1913, did more damage than any other weather event, destroying 11 commercial boats and killing 250 men with a stroke on Lake Huron. These frightful freshwater death-rolls are little remembered down the decades – almost certainly because all of them happened in the age before television, before the immediacy of the electronic media in promulgating the bad news (and the hit song).

They are, nonetheless, equally worth of commemoration, in a doleful countdown.

Eastland

The very worst loss of life on the Great Lakes? Incredibly, it took place on a placid summer day, not during one of the notorious November storms. It happened not on the open water, but in a river inlet of a major city, surrounded by lifesaving personnel and rescuers at the ready. It happened in water one could easily swim. It robbed at least 836 people of their lives in minutes.

Early on Saturday, July 24, 1915, the passenger steamer *Eastland* sat in the Chicago River, waiting to convey a full load of merrymakers from Chicago and across Lake Michigan to a popular annual picnic among the sand dunes of Michigan City, Indiana. The *Eastland* packet steamer launched in 1903 on the Black River of Port Huron, Michigan. She had been designed to engage in the competitive pleasure-excursion market of the era, with oak paneling and mahogany parlors, two levels of observation decks, numerous staterooms, a saloon, and a steam calliope. She could supposedly carry up to 3,300 passengers in addition to her crew of 70.

For this particular trip to the famous Indiana dunes, more than 7,300 tickets had been sold. Most of the customers were employees and families connected with the giant Western Electric Company. About 3,500 people packed aboard the *Eastland*'s decks shortly after 7 a.m., when the steamship pulled away from the pier on the Chicago River. A second steamer, the *Theodore Roosevelt*, waited to take the overflow crowds to the picnic. The picnic never took place.

The *Eastland* had long been rumored, in previous passenger runs from Cleveland to Cedar Point in Sandusky, and from Chicago to South Haven, to be an unstable vessel. Modifications in her engines early in her career, plus a decision to make her a shallow-draft vessel – riding higher in the water to navigate the lesser fathoms of rivers and pleasure-boat piers – had left her top-heavy, with a distinct inclination to tilt. In one 1904 excursion, ferrying Chicago postal workers to South Haven, the accumulation of sightseers on the topmost level or "hurricane" deck gave the ship such a list that the crew feared she might capsize. When passengers ignored orders to go below and stabilize the ship's center of gravity, desperate crewmen turned a firehose on them.

Despite the poor word-of-mouth stirred by this portent, owners of the *Eastland* claimed their business was merely the target of slander by rival pleasure-boat syndicates, and offered $5,000 to anyone who could prove the *Eastland* unseaworthy. There were no challengers. In 1914 and 1915, furthermore, the *Eastland* underwent renovations, partially in response to safety precautions instituted throughout the passenger-boat industry after the loss of the *Titanic*. More lifeboats were added, as were more life vests, and a wooden upper floor rotted from years of spilled beverage was replaced with concrete. But these "improvements" had the effect of making the ship only more unstable.

Thus, on July 24, did the incomprehensible unfold in a light rain, in one of the modern cities in the world. Almost immediately after casting off, the *Eastland* began to list to port, then to starboard, rocking beneath the top-heavy crush of human cargo, with the chief engineer Joe Erickson unable to compensate with the ballast tanks. Some reports cite a particular catalyst for the calamity – a photographer, prominently set up with his tripod and picture-taking apparatus on one bank of the river; passengers saw him and rushed en masse to one side of the vessel to have their image captured.

In any case, the ship began a steep, irreversible lean to port. Crew tried to herd passengers to the starboard, but the gradient was too steep. A piano and a refrigerator toppled and slid to collide with a bulkhead and people. At approximately 7:30 a.m., the *Eastland* half overturned in the twenty-foot-deep Chicago River, casting hundreds into the water and trapping others in the flooded hull. The lifejackets, intended to avert another *Titanic*, were stowed away in locked wooden containers over the passenger compartments – inaccessible.

Distress and deaths surrounding the half-submerged steamer would keep headline-writers busy as the scale of the calamity unfolded. Men kept a firm hold on the boat with one hand while trying to keep women from drowning with the other, hoisting them by their hair. A teenage Western Electric employee, just chosen beauty queen of the plant, died in one of the cabins. A fireman involved in rescue efforts discovered the sodden corpse of his own little daughter among the dead. Many entire families had joined the Western Electric excursion; someone calculated that twenty-two households were completely annihilated.

The *Eastland*'s captain, Harry Pedersen, possibly dazed from a blow to the head as the ship turned over, quarreled and interfered with the lifesavers who started cutting into the hull with acetylene torches. Police arrested him – then had to protect him from an angry mob. Later, a US District Attorney would order arrests of twenty-seven further crew.

Bodies of the dead recovered – some estimates went as high as 852, but 836 is a figure that tallies with the records – were all conveyed to makeshift morgues. The city's own facilities were not remotely large enough to cope. Wicker baskets had to hold bodies when caskets ran short. Corpses filled the 2nd Regiment Armory Building on Washington Street, and they were numbered and lain on the floor in rows of 85, to make identification easier for surviving family members (if any). A number of ghost stories are told about those buildings today: phantom women in archaic-style clothing; the sound of sobbing heard with no identifiable source.

Mass funerals in Chicago and Cicero, where most of the Western Electric employees lived, took place the next Wednesday. By the end of July, multiple inquests and trials convened to determine who was at fault. Once again, the owners denied the *Eastland* had safety issues; they blamed Captain Pedersen – who, in turn, blamed Chief Engineer Erickson, who would be defended in court by legendary lawyer Clarence Darrow.

Darrow claimed that a sudden movement of passengers to one side had indeed tilted the *Eastland* past the point Erickson's ballast-tanks could balance her. The excursionists, in this defense, were said to be watching another passing boat, not posing for a photo. But some survivors countered that they were crammed so tightly on board that no such mass-migration had even been possible. Accusations came that the 75-cent tickets were so aggressively foisted upon Western Electric Company employees that many felt they had no choice but buy them and join the doomed voyage, lest they lose their jobs, a climate of fear that management denied fostering.

Pedersen also stated that the steamship had hitched up on an unknown underwater obstruction. Later, a local diver, William "Frenchy" Deneau (see Chapter 7), would seem to reinforce Pedersen, saying he had found rubble and pilings on the river bottom. And still later, Deneau would retract. The court cases and finger-pointing dragged on for decades. Ultimately Captain Pedersen and the rest of the crew were exonerated. Pedersen never commanded another ship again, while Joe Erickson died at age 37 in 1919 of heart disease.

When the case finally reached its conclusion in 1935, the verdict rather conveniently faulted Erickson, now beyond the reach of earthly justice or the defense of Clarence Darrow, as having been lax – not the owners or the inspectors. After the salvage costs and vessel expenses, the amount of damages paid out and divided among victims' families from the sale value was ridiculous – about $10,000. One may find a degree of sympathy with the predictable complaints of the steamship workers' trade union, that it was all profiteering, collusion, and coverup between company owners and the government.

Yet the *Eastland* affair, except for legal entanglements, largely receded from the public mind. A recent author dubbed the Chicago River disaster "America's forgotten tragedy," and it is worth contrasting the *Eastland*'s relative obscurity against another ghastly incident in which company profits played a dubious role – the storied 1911 Triangle Shirtwaist Factory fire in New York City, in which 145 were killed. With America's entry into WWI, the *Eastland* herself was refurbished for the United States Navy as a home-front gunship and bore the name *Wilmette*. The Chicago River mayhem seemed to have left no mark of shame upon the *Wilmette*, as she carried President Franklin Delano Roosevelt and his cabinet, among other dignitaries, as a largely ceremonial Great Lakes military vessel. The *Wilmette* was finally cut up for scrap in 1947.

Not until June 9, 1989, was a plaque installed at the edge of the Chicago River honoring the fatalities. That has been the lone permanent memorial – until the recent establishment of the *Eastland* Disaster Historical Society, an organization founded by two granddaughters of Borghild Amelia Decker Carlson, one of the longest-lived survivors of the capsizing. Borghild had been thrown from the starboard side, and an uncle helped hold her head above water. She died in 1991.

The *Eastland* Disaster Historical Society anticipates the centennial of the tragedy on July 25, 2015, with far more ceremony than the barren decades during which the anniversary passed utterly unrecognized. And, in the summer of 2012, Chicago's Lookingglass Theatre premiered an original stage musical about the *Eastland*.

While the legalese might argue that the *Eastland* affair was a river disaster, not a lake one, it is counted among the ledgers of lives lost to Lake Michigan. And, of all the Great Lakes, Michigan's death toll adds up to the highest, worse even than fearsomely storm-tossed and abyssal Superior.

It is a bit of a statistical fluke, lopsided by the *Eastland* sum coupled with another devastating Lake Michigan event, the 1860 collision of the *Augusta* and the *Lady Elgin*.

Augusta and Lady Elgin

The *Augusta* was a 128-foot cargo schooner, hauling a load of pine out of Oswego under Captain Darius Malott. The *Lady Elgin*, for her part, was an attractive 252-foot sidewheel steamer, launched in 1851 and originally Canadian owned and named for the wife of the governor of Canada. Affectionately called "the Queen of the Lakes" for her handsome appearance and popularity with Great Lakes excursionists, she still had a mild reputation for bad luck, the proverbial "jinx ship."

What luck she did have ran out September 7. The steamer, under Captain John Wilson, embarked from Milwaukee with a crowd of revelers affiliated with the Union Guards. This was a former federal military organization that had been forced to disband by Wisconsin Governor Alexander Randall, an ardent Abolitionist who had threatened to remove Wisconsin from the Union entirely if slavery were not soon abolished; he perceived the Union Guards as the long arm of a Washington, D.C., still on the wrong side of the slavery issue. The Union Guards, proud soldiers and veterans, sought to keep themselves together via self-financing, and to that end they had sold tickets for a *Lady Elgin* pleasure cruise to their many friends and supporters among Milwaukee's Irish-American and Democratic Party community. Nobody was sure, in the end, how many passengers were on board, but they probably numbered close to 400. Their destination was Chicago, for a day in the great city, followed by a banquet on board the ship in the evening.

With bad weather threatening, Captain Wilson deliberated over whether to spend the night docked in Chicago for refuge, but he was finally persuaded to embark for Milwaukee at 11:30 p.m. On the way back home, a thunderstorm began, but it did not dissuade partygoers still dancing on the decks to a live band. Meanwhile, in the same overcast, inclement darkness, was the *Augusta*, sailing in a tempest without running lights.

At 2 a.m., both ships came within visual range of each other – or what passed for visual range, given the rain and the occasional flashes of lightning. The men of the *Augusta*, fighting to keep their sails in order, discerned the illumination of the much larger *Lady Elgin*, but their view was obscured by stacks of lumber on their decks and they could not determine her course in time. When Captain Malott realized a collision was imminent, he ordered a turn to starboard, but it was too late. At about 2:30 a.m., the schooner pierced the *Lady Elgin* amidships at her gangplank, right beside her giant paddlewheel. For a brief time, the riggings of the *Augusta* tangled in debris of the *Lady Elgin*, the Queen of the Lakes dragging the smaller ship along, but they separated.

Captain Malott and his crew prepared for the worst when they inspected their vessel, but were surprised to find the *Augusta*, though shaken, still seaworthy, with manageable leaks. As for the *Lady Elgin*, she seemed to be continuing unperturbed on her way, so the schooner's crew proceeded to turn their attention to getting to Chicago, reporting the incident and patching themselves up. It is recorded that they were rather offended that the *Lady Elgin* had not stopped to inquire if the *Augusta* needed assistance.

But, in fact, the majestic *Lady Elgin* was the ship in mortal jeopardy. Though the tapered deck of the *Augusta* had speared her well above the waterline, the breach extended much farther down than Malott had thought, inundating the lower decks. Further battered by the waves, she tried to make for shore but her decks collapsed and her steam-turbine engines plunged through the hole. Two out of her four lifeboats were launched – one of them actually filled with crew members, allegedly dispatched by Captain Wilson to see if the gap in the hull could be patched from the outside, perhaps with mattresses. Instead, the lifeboat swamped in the rough seas. The *Lady Elgin* sank with stunning rapidity, about ten miles from shore off Winnetka, her entire top "hurricane" deck separating and providing survivors, including Captain Wilson, with a largish makeshift life-raft – for a time.

Wind and waves started to break the hurricane deck apart, but the largest section, by daybreak, had floated within a few hundred feet of the shore at Evanston. It was not a gently sloping, sandy beach, however, but a rocky cliff-face, and half of the passengers clinging to the deck lost their lives here in the angry surf.

In one of the few mercies of that morning, the first of the two lifeboats had, amazingly, kept afloat, reached the same rocky beach safely, and delivered the crewmen, who immediately summoned help from shore-dwellers, including a lifesaving crew from the school that would later become Northwestern University. Still, many could do little as the remnants of the *Lady Elgin* eddied and roiled in the waves. Captain Wilson drowned, reportedly in the act of trying to rescue a woman from the water.

In Milwaukee, so they say, a police officer in those early-morning hours found himself unable to sleep and felt pulled by a nameless dread to make a house-to-house inspection of his beat – the predominantly Irish Third Ward, where many of the Union Guard families, supporters, and Democrats lived. It was as though he had sensed the enormity of what was happening on Lake Michigan. Official counts gave the number of dead at 297, but due to last-minute cancellations and changes to the passenger roster, an exact total of casualties has been argued and could have been as high as 350. For the large families of Irish-Americans in both Milwaukee and Chicago, by one estimate, the accident created no less than a thousand orphans, in what would remain for more than a half-century the single worst loss of life on the Great Lakes – until the *Eastland*.

An inquest began at once, and indeed down to this day maritime buffs and historians still try to determine guilt and responsibility. The trial divulged that the *Lady Elgin* had been built without watertight hull bulkhead compartments, a recent safety measure that could very well have kept her afloat. Captain Wilson, having died a hero's death, was less singled out for blame than Captain Malott, even though the *Lady Elgin* had, more or less, failed to yield for a commercial vessel as she should have. The official verdict – that neither ship could be held at fault – satisfied no one. Milwaukee's anger would later fall upon the *Augusta* herself, now considered a "ship killer," an Irish mob besieging her when she docked in Milwaukee. The schooner's owners, Bissel & Davidson, subsequently repainted the hull, changed her name to the *Colonel Cook* and sold her to another company. Under the new owners, she sank on Lake Erie three times in four years, each time salvaged and put back into service until a final, definitive collision with a Cleveland-area breakwall wrecked her beyond repair in 1894. Darius Malott, meanwhile, continued to skipper for Bissel & Davidson. In 1864, he and nine crewman, most of them from the *Augusta*, all vanished somewhere in Lake Michigan with their ship, the *Mojave*.

While the *Eastland* disaster was strangely forgotten, the fatal account of the *Augusta* and the *Lady Elgin* has lived on as Milwaukee-Chicago lore. Relics of the sinking that drifted ashore (including a piano, reportedly haunted) dot local museums and collections. Like the *Edmund Fitzgerald* there was a popular song written to commemorate the tragedy, "Lost on the *Lady Elgin*." It came from the pen of Henry C. Work, who also wrote the standards "Grandfather's Clock" and "Marching through Georgia" (see Afterword Part II).

Pewabic and *Meteor*

Modern author Mark L. Thompson has made a book-length study of disasters of the Great Lakes. In his judgment, the title for worst ship-to-ship collision in the history of the inland seas was not the *Augusta/Lady Elgin*, however. In terms of a staggeringly preventable tragedy, Thompson awards the notoriety to the deadly Lake Huron dance of the *Pewabic* and the *Meteor*.

These were sister ships proudly built by J.B. Whiting & Co. of Detroit, as two 225-foot combination passenger steamship and cargo freighters. They had elegant rosewood staterooms and stained-glass salons able to accommodate up to 400 passengers. Whiting's ships enjoyed notable success on the Great Lakes, and the *Pewabic*, by reputation, could boast the best safety features money could buy. It was not enough.

On August 9, 1865, the *Pewabic*, under Captain George McKay, steamed underway with 350 tons (some sources report 500 tons) of copper ingots from the mines of Michigan's Keweenaw Peninsula, plus other freight and about 200 tourists – the number of pleasure-trip customers increasing with the conclusion of the Civil War – bound for Cleveland. She was on Huron off Thunder Bay at dusk when she fatally crossed paths with her very own sister ship *Meteor*, heading for Sault Ste. Marie out of Detroit, with Captain Thomas Wilson at the helm.

In fine weather, with clear visibility and no apparent malfunction, the *Meteor* and *Pewabic* drew close to each other in an apparent maneuver to pass side-by-side. Then, at about 6:30 p.m., the *Meteor* smashed into the *Pewabic*'s port side, striking several yards from the bow.

The impact killed many of the passengers outright, and the shattered ship sank in a mere five minutes, off Alpena, Michigan. The death toll of 125 would have been much higher had not Captain Thomas Wilson swung the undamaged *Meteor* expertly alongside and rescued virtually everyone who could move off the submerging *Pewabic*. Captain McKay helped with the evacuation, though he was delayed with putting out a fire that had started in one of the *Pewabic*'s plush smoking rooms, as lit cigarettes tipped over.

Later, both captains were praised for their heroism, and enjoyed long Great Lakes maritime careers, even with outrage in the news media and the evidence of a post-accident inquest suggesting both ships at fault, to varying degrees. It seemed they had sought to try to pass each other at the narrowest possible approach – when no navigation hazards made such a tight sea-lane necessary. In fact, the inquiry concluded that it was the *Pewabic* that had veered most off-course, putting herself irrevocably in the oncoming *Meteor*'s trajectory, apparently overcompensating at the last minute to get out of her sister's way. Captain McKay's master's license was revoked after the inquest, but later restored on appeal.

What exactly brought the two ships into such close quarters remained unanswered, though there have been suggestions that one or both ships might have been trying to engage in a routine, albeit dangerous maneuver, of passing so close to one another that mailbags and recent newspapers could be simply tossed by the sailors from one deck to another. Soon more stringent maritime regulations would curtail such risky behaviors.

In a morbid sequel to the *Pewabic* sinking, the lost ship continued to steal lives. Rumors claimed the wreck held, in addition to a fortune in copper, $50,000 in gold on board in a strongbox, with possibly greater riches in a mysterious secondary safe, still in the hulk 175 feet below Lake Huron's surface. Several early divers, in ungainly, dangerous iron suits and clumsy air hoses, died searching for the *Pewabic*, prior to the wreck being firmly located in 1897. That she was found sitting on even keel on the bottom tempted future treasure-hunters, with increasingly better technology for deep-water retrievals. But still one after another was defeated by water and weather. In 1914, a diving-bell expedition went down to the *Pewabic* – but it flooded in the depths. When raised to the surface, it only brought the bodies of both men who had been inside. So the *Pewabic*'s grim toll of 125 perhaps requires an asterisk.

Finally, a well-funded 1917 expedition by the Leavitt Deep Sea Diving Company succeeded in reaching the *Pewabic* and harvesting most of what she had to offer. Allegedly, the staterooms held the bones and skeletons of those 1865 pleasure-seekers who never had the chance to disembark. Copper ingots and relics were recovered, while the enticing fortune that had drawn a handful more to their deaths proved to have been paper money – now decomposed to worthlessness.

The approach of a steamer in the 1800s was an inspiring sight – and, on occasion, a fatal one. *1898 Motograph Moving Picture Book.*

Atlantic and Ogdensburgh

Another devastating collision was that which took place in the predawn hours on Lake Erie on August 20, 1852. The *Atlantic* was a "palace steamer," 267 feet long and operated by the mighty Michigan Central Railroad. She was intended to be as much a beauty to behold on the water as one of that company's passenger trains might be at a depot. There was a commercial rather than aesthetic reason for such luxury, of course. She and other steamers like her vied for a clientele of immigrants headed westward in the land rushes and settlements of the mid-1800s. Such transports that catered to immigrant business in eastern ports like Buffalo were dolled up to be the proverbial "ship of dreams" to bear the newcomers into the heartland.

In her case, the *Atlantic* bid to be one of the fastest, promising a Buffalo-to-Detroit run – a 261-mile route – in less than seventeen hours.

Thus, was she carrying about 600 immigrant passengers west when, at about 2 a.m., she passed the notoriously treacherous Long Point on the north shore of Lake Erie. Approaching from west to east, however, was the steam-powered freighter *Ogdensburgh* bearing a cargo of wheat to her namesake city of Ogdensburgh, New York. Portentously, her warning-whistle was not functioning.

Aboard the *Ogdensburgh*, First Mate Degrass McNell sighted the *Atlantic* and judged there to be no danger. However, the *Atlantic* started to veer into *Ogdensburgh*'s path. Though the freighter took evasive action, the two ships closed in each other, the bow of the *Ogdensburgh* ramming into the *Atlantic*'s port side.

The incident summoned the *Ogdensburgh*'s Captain Robert Richardson from his bunk. After determining that his own steamer was still seaworthy, he followed the *Atlantic* – not making the same mistake that the *Augusta* would with the *Lady Elgin* – suspecting the worst. Sure enough, the other ship was taking on water badly. The collision had awakened some of the passengers, but the crew were recorded as being of no assistance whatsoever; it was literally a free-for-all panic, and the boat began listing to port, and more and more human waves of groggy travelers, many without English-language skills, came up with their families from their sleeping quarters.

People threw anything that could float into Lake Erie to try and escape the *Atlantic* – and it seems that assurances that deck furniture could be used as flotation devices were badly exaggerated. Fortunately, the weather was calm, and the *Ogdensburgh* maneuvered aside the stricken *Atlantic* to take some 200 people aboard. Other ships came to assist, as the *Atlantic* drowned and settled to the muddy lake bottom several miles south of the Canadian shoreline.

Much as it has become a repeated aphorism, the motto "women and children first," has its origin in British seafaring tradition. There is a name for it, the "Birkenhead Drill," after the 1852 incident in which twenty wives were taken off the floundering *HMS Birkenhead* in the sole lifeboat while their men stayed behind, an act of valor commemorated by Rudyard Kipling in verse. Yet, for all the clichés, the Birkenhead Drill was not law – and has been seldom observed in practice (the *Titanic* being one of the few cases the command actually was given and followed). It certainly was not the case with the *Atlantic*. Later, it would be learned that the Captain and his crew had hastily seen themselves off the vessel in its only two lifeboats and one extra boat, apparently not even bothering to determine if all the sleeping immigrants had at least evacuated the lower decks. Because of poor record-keeping, the exact toll of those who died in Lake Erie that night varies, somewhere between 130 and 250 casualties.

Walk-in-the-Water and Erie

The combination of immigrants and steamship-engine technology would account for several epochal tragedies during this era, requiring no colliding freighter or intruding schooner to deal a deadly blow.

The first Great Lakes steamship was a 135-foot vessel called *Walk-in-the-Water*, who made her appearance on Lake Erie in 1818, presenting a profile much like a regular brigantine with full sales, augmented by a "sidewheel" wood-burning, steam-driven paddle. She perished when a November gale beat her to pieces on Lake Erie only three years later, but all aboard were rescued. Two decades later, in 1837, the *Erie* launched. She was a more streamlined, 176-foot passenger steamer considered in her construction to be an exceptionally refined vessel, true state-of-the-art for the new propulsion method.

After four years of service, in the summer of 1841, the *Erie*'s hull was given a new coat of whitewash and varnish. She was immaculate as she left Buffalo on August 9, under the command of Captain Thomas J. Titus, bound for her namesake port city of Erie, Pennsylvania, with Chicago as the ultimate destination. She carried more than 250 passengers, many of them newly arrived immigrants from Swiss and German regions. One passenger even brought a prized race horse aboard.

As with the later supreme example of the *Titanic*, a case may be made for reckless pride in the fall of the *Erie*. The painting and cosmetic refinishing intended to make the ship look her finest also meant that large quantities of turpentine and other accelerants were on board – along with some of the painting contractors, headed towards a new job in Erie.

Nobody knows conclusively if the fresh coatings and inflammables carried by the *Erie* caused the ghastly fire that swept the ship. Great Lakes historian Dwight Boyer has stated as fact that the painters left their turpentine in demijons on deck, at a spot fatefully above the hot boilers. Others have conjectured that, regardless of the painters, the boilers exploded. Either way, around twilight, a fireball tore through the decks as the *Erie* floated forty miles west of Buffalo. The painters' chemicals unquestionably fed the blaze, which seemed to originate around the smokestacks. A Lake Erie breeze fanned the spreading tongues of flame across the ship.

At this point in American powered sea transportation, regular inspections, on-board engineers and firehoses and pumps were mandatory under the law. But the idea of fire drills and other passenger-safety precautions were ill-favored or ignored – certainly nothing on which the companies in the excursion and freight business wasted valuable time and effort. Captain Titus tried to herd the panicking passengers to the lifeboats, but with little success. He ordered helmsman Augustus Fuller – some sources give the name as Luther Fuller – to man the wheel and make for the New York shore as quickly as possible. Fuller obeyed, to the last. He remained in the pilothouse as flames incinerated it.

A later inquest would lay out the true scale of the tragedy. Due to rough waves, many of the passengers, especially women and children, had retired for the night to their cabins, where the conflagration trapped them. No children – and only one woman – survived out of more than a hundred on board. As the steam pressure dropped from the devastated engines, the ship stalled – and the course-change toward shore mainly achieved putting the vessel at a fresh angle to the wind that allowed the flames to scour any wood and painted surface not already being consumed. Lifejackets had been stored near the smokestacks and were destroyed early.

People not already lost to the flames took their chances in the water. Captain Titus managed to launch a yawl as a lifeboat, but the crush of frenzied passengers and crew overturned it. He saved himself by clinging to the upturned boat. Others grabbed onto anything that could float – that was not burning. Only twenty-seven survived.

Within two hours of the explosion, another steamship, the *Dewitt Clinton*, spotted the glow of the fire and picked up the survivors. Other ships responded as well and tried to tow the burning wreck to shore, but the remains of the *Erie* instead broke apart and went to the bottom off Silver Creek, in sixty feet of water. Salvors would later pick through her remains to find – and cash – the silver and gold coin and trinkets brought over by the immigrants, the seed money that had melted into lumps.

It is possible that the *Erie* is the Great Lakes disaster that has had more fame and influence than the *Edmund Fitzgerald* – just not under the right names. For the side detail of Augustus Fuller's death while dutifully at the wheel, executing his captain's final instruction, caught the imagination of various popular writers. Charles Dickens, during an 1842 journey across Lake Erie he found personally disagreeable (see Chapter 2), heard the account and fictionalized the sacrifice in a short story, "The Helmsman of Lake Erie," which changed the ship's name to *Jersey*. He also altered Helmsman Fuller to "John Maynard" and changed numerous other details.

Still, it seems the widely published Dickens story was accepted by many readers as unadulterated fact. Horatio Alger Jr. made the death of John Maynard into a ballad (now calling the stricken vessel the *Ocean Queen*). A European poet, Theodor Fontane, recycled the whole incident yet again, redubbing the burning ship the *Swallow* and rewriting history to the extent that every human being on board her disembarked safe and sound – except for John Maynard, who gave himself to the flames and was honored by a marble monument with gold lettering in Buffalo, ultimate commemoration of his ultimate sacrifice.

By the mid-20th-century – in the German-speaking parts of Europe especially – the much-retold legend of John Maynard had gained a stature equal to that of heroic locomotive engineer Casey Jones. On more than one occasion, German tourists and exchange students lodging near Lake Erie have been astounded and disappointed to learn that none of their American hosts had ever heard of the great John Maynard, the man who placed duty above all mortal concerns. In 1997, however, the city of Buffalo, with their German sister-city of Dortmund, did unveil a plaque in the Erie Basin Marina in memory of the *Erie*, the poet Fontane, and "John Maynard," whoever he might be.

As, sadly, the name of Augustus/Luther Fuller is now unknown to most. And there is a strange postscript to his story, that one of the other crewman in the *Erie*'s pilothouse, who had escaped the blaze, lived out the rest of his life as a town drunk. Yet another crewman began circulating spurious claims that the drunk was, in fact, *Fuller himself*. The heroic pilot, according to the slander, had deserted his post after all, taken an assumed name and drunk himself into the grave out of shame and guilt.

The entire twisted saga is far removed from the verses that have been memorized and recited by generations of German schoolchildren, to this very day (see Afterword Part III). As translated by Julie and Amy Huberman of Buffalo, New York:

The city has its tribute shown:
"Here lies John Maynard! In smoke and fire
He held fast to the wheel; he did not tire.
He saved our lives, our noble king.
He died for us; his praise we sing.
John Maynard!"

The demise of the *Erie* brought no immediate reform in steamship procedure or safety; there would have to be further infernos.

Phoenix

It is a minor aspect of superstition on the Great Lakes that naming a ship after a bird is bad luck – and naming a ship *Phoenix* especially inadvisable. Several *Phoenixes* are recorded as having met their ends on the inland seas, sometimes, ironically, by fire. The mythological phoenix arises again from the pile of its own ashes. The one that embarked from Buffalo on November 11, 1847, did not.

This *Phoenix* was a 155-foot steamer carrying cargoes of coffee, molasses, sugar – and Dutch immigrants from the Netherlands being the overwhelming majority of her 275 passengers. Their transport was to have been the final run of the *Phoenix* for the season, and the circuit from the start proved a bad one.

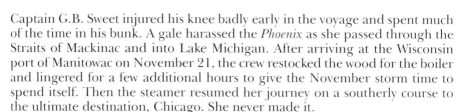

Captain G.B. Sweet injured his knee badly early in the voyage and spent much of the time in his bunk. A gale harassed the *Phoenix* as she passed through the Straits of Mackinac and into Lake Michigan. After arriving at the Wisconsin port of Manitowac on November 21, the crew restocked the wood for the boiler and lingered for a few additional hours to give the November storm time to spend itself. Then the steamer resumed her journey on a southerly course to the ultimate destination, Chicago. She never made it.

At 4 a.m. in the morning, on November 22, smoke began pouring out of the firehold, where the overheated engine boilers had set the *Phoenix* herself aflame. The Dutch passengers in steerage noticed the calamity first, and their panic brought the ship's engineer and fireman to try, vainly, to put out the blaze. As the engine room turned to ashes, the ship's power died, and the burning *Phoenix* was helpless in the water, four miles from shore between Manitowac and Sheboygan.

Attempts by the crew to form a bucket brigade and quench the fire met obstacles with the eruption on deck of one panicked Dutch family after another, many not knowing any English. That made doubly impossible the dilemma faced by the injured Captain Sweet, that the *Phoenix* carried only two lifeboats, each with a maximum capacity of twenty. The best he and his crew could offer hundreds of terror-stricken immigrants was to attempt to row the two boats in relays through the November surf to the beach and back. By the time the two packed boats arrived, the oarsmen were exhausted and virtually paralyzed with cold, and nobody cared to go back.

The *Phoenix* blazed like a Viking pyre on Lake Michigan, some of its doomed human cargo leaping into the freezing lake, others trying to find relief on the higher decks and the masts themselves. Other ships saw the inferno in the distance and came to offer help. The steamer *Delaware* found only three left alive – a trio of crewmen who took a chance that the rudder chain would not burn and offered the only handhold on the *Phoenix* that was survivable. The *Delaware* brought the men and the burned-out shell of the ship into Sheboygan.

Out of about 300 men, women, and children on board the *Phoenix*, 258 had perished. Afterwards, according to the histories, in-shore souvenir merchants made a macabre profit selling countless wooden clogs that they claimed had washed up on shore, footwear lost by the doomed Netherlanders aboard the *Phoenix*. It is also said that an entrepreneurial Sheboygan native, plumbing the depths of the charred *Phoenix* after the corpses had all been removed, discovered all the gold and jewels that the immigrants had brought with them – melted into one lump or vein. This discovery gave him the startup funds to buy a few cows from Ohio and start the first dairy farm in Sheboygan.

G.P. Griffith

On a larger scale in the world of commerce, the lack of proper lifeboats, safety drills, or boiler supervision aboard the *Phoenix* – or for that matter, the *Erie* – led to no modifications, legislation, or reforms. The companies strongly resisted them, even as further steamer explosions and fires occurred, some with just "minor" loss of life – twenty-nine dead in the case of the *Troy* blowing up in Buffalo, New York, thirty-eight with the *Anthony Wayne* igniting off Vermilion, Ohio, both in 1850. But it would take the addition of the three-figure casualties of the *G.P. Griffith*, that same year on Lake Erie, to finally bring about even a semblance of regulations for steamers.

Built on the Maumee River in 1847, she was a wooden "packet steamer," named for the memorably monikered Griffith P. Griffith, founder of the Troy and Erie Transportation Line shipping company. Propelled by two paddlewheels 31 feet in diameter, the white-painted steamer was 193 feet long, sporting luxurious accommodations above the cargo hold, with French-influenced décor in the 56 staterooms (some of them full suites with double beds and their own parlors).

On June 16, 1850, she cast off with 356 passengers, mostly immigrants who had come aboard at Buffalo intending to settle in Cleveland and other cities to the west. Also on board were the wife, mother, and children of Captain Charles Roby, enjoying what was intended to be a pleasant summer run headed west.

Just before Cleveland, the ship stopped at Fairport Harbor to take on two additional crew. There is an account that one of the men complained of smelling smoke and was brusquely told by a crew member to ignore it. But in the early hours of June 17, the ship's wheelsman saw sparks flying upward from the "air jackets," a sort of vent around the smokestacks rising out of the decks from the boiler-room. Pouring water into the air jackets had no effect; the sparks soon became sheets of flame. Clearly a major blaze was burning through the ship's heart.

Captain Roby tried to make for the shore, coming within three miles of the neighborhood of Willoughby, east of Cleveland, when the flames burst out on deck. He brought the dying ship a mile and half from the shore – which bore scant illumination and certainly no lighthouses – when the *G.P. Griffith* grounded in sandy shallows, on a bar about eight feet below the surface, in water still too deep for the passengers to safely disembark.

It was utter bedlam. Some passengers flung themselves off the steamer as it made for shore only to be chewed up in the paddlewheels. Others died by fire, while most drowned. Chief Engineer David Stebbins earned honors for himself by swimming to shore, commandeering a skiff, and paddling back to the burning *Griffith* to save anyone he could. He made this trip three times.

In the end, there were only 42 survivors, meaning 287 dead – including Captain Roby and his family. Dawn drew hundreds to the scene of the disaster, the smoking wreck with askew smokestacks still standing. At least one local resident claimed that many of the visitors – specifically from the metropolis of Cleveland, not pastoral Willoughby – were lured by rumors that the dead immigrants had carried small fortunes with them in their clothes, and that coins and gold could be easily scavenged. And indeed, according to J.E. Hopkins, a local historian who has researched the *Griffith*, money is distinctly absent in the list of personal possessions salvaged from the victims and temporarily stored in an area barn.

OHIO HISTORICAL MARKER

THE *GRIFFITH* DISASTER, 1850

Following the completion of the Erie Canal from Albany to Buffalo, New York, Lake Erie became an important link in an all-water route for immigrants traveling from the eastern seaboard into the Midwest. The 600-ton lake steamer *G.P. Griffith*, launched in 1847, was one of dozens built to capitalize on this booming trade. On June 17, 1850, the *Griffith*, outbound with more than 300 passengers on a three-day voyage from Buffalo to Toledo, caught fire and burned about 220 yards from this overlook. Many of the German, English, Irish, and Scandinavian settlers were laden with money sewn into their clothing, and few reached shore. Contemporary accounts listed 286 lost. Most were buried in a mass grave on the beach, since reclaimed by Lake Erie. The *Griffith* incident remains one of the worst maritime disasters on the Great Lakes.

THE OHIO BICENTENNIAL COMMISSION
THE LONGABERGER COMPANY
LAKE METROPARKS
CITY OF WILLOWICK
THE LAKE COUNTY HISTORICAL SOCIETY
THE OHIO HISTORICAL SOCIETY
2000

9-43

On a once-tragic stretch of Lake Erie beach, a plaque in a public park now commemorates the *G.P. Griffith*.

Many of the corpses were laid out on the beach for easy identification by what family members or friends could do the grim task. In the end, however, many unclaimed, anonymous bodies were buried in one mass grave on the hills above the shore. Although various community groups, almost from the beginning, argued over what to do with the land in which the dead were interred, J.E. Hopkins writes that very likely the bodies were just ignored. The land was later developed into Willoughbeach Park, one of greater Cleveland's many amusement funfairs of yesteryear. Published accounts from the 1920s include an article claiming one of Willoughbeach's maintenance-workers regularly inspected the park grounds for pieces of bone protruding from the ground; he was charged with secretly removing and disposing of the remains before any revelers saw them.

On what caused the fire of the *G.P. Griffith*, there were divergent theories. One was that Chief Engineer Stebbins was trying a new engine-oil lubricant with an unfortunately low burning point, and this he unwisely stored in drums in the engine room itself. Another theory was that a large quantity of matches was among the cargo carried by the ship, and that load ignited. Or perhaps there was a dust-explosion and fire owing to the quantity of grain aboard.

Of course, the obvious suggestion is that the engine, or more precisely, its boilers, caught fire through poor maintenance. One survivor would much later claim – and be the only one to do so – that Captain Roby was careless about safety and actually pushed the *G.P. Griffith* beyond her tolerances to race a rival steamboat, a situation common on lakes and rivers during the steam age and often cause for on-board explosions. J.E. Hopkins was dissatisfied with these suppositions and accusations, and he ruminates that the cause could have been as mundane as a dropped cigarette by one of the passengers; we will never know for certain.

After the *Griffith* immolation – remember, just the third major steamship disaster on the Great Lakes in one year – the United States Congress enacted the Steamboat Act of 1852. It specifically attacked practices of installing underpowered or inferior steam boilers as a cost-cutting measure, and it formalized a Steamboat Inspection Service (which, in 1915, was merged into the US Coast Guard), putting more teeth into the existing laws.

Even so, tragedies continued to happen on the Five Sisters. From the more than a hundred (the exact number uncertain) killed when a fast-moving fire of undetermined cause swept the steamer *Seabird* on April 8, 1868, during a Milwaukee-to-Chicago transit; to the 31 out of the 33-man crew of the 639-foot cargo freighter *Carl Bradley* who drowned after the colossal ship broke apart in a Lake Michigan storm on November 18, 1958.

As old-timers may tell you, when the bells ring 29 times on every November 10, they are not ringing exclusively for the lost crew of the *Edmund Fitzgerald*, but for all those, ships and men, named and nameless, whose lives have been snatched away on the Five Sisters.

The mythic "Diana of the Dunes" *au naturel* in her natural element on the Indiana beaches fronting Lake Michigan. This rendition, a tribute to the style of Maxfield Parrish, was done by Chip Karpus, an Ohio-based multimedia artist and filmmaker. *Courtesy of Chip Karpus.*

Ghosts in the Marine

In Which the Treats, Habits and Likenesses of After-Death Spirits and Apparitions of the Great Lakes are Detailed and Discussed. The Bannockburn's *Position as Fleet-Leader Challenged by a Chicago Schooner with a Santa Claus Connection. Deceased Lighthouse Personnel Shown to Possess Extraordinary Tenacity or Job Security. Lake Michigan's "Seaweed Charlie" Bids Fair to Be the Most Oft-Seen Ghost in History, Whilst Few Eyes Can Be Found Who Admit to Ogling Diana of the Dunes. The Most Famous Great Lakes Ghost May Not Have Existed (Which Skeptics May Judge a Redundant Statement).*

I n the 1970s, a beloved grandfather once made a gift to me of a book which, in many ways, inspired the one you are now holding. It was Dwight Boyer's 1968 *Ghost Ships of the Great Lakes.*

Boyer first opened my mind to the wealth of stories and legends of the Five Sisters, and yet my younger self found *Ghost Ships of the Great Lakes*, with its evocative sea-green cover illustration of a drowned freighter, somewhat frustrating.

Dwight Boyer, a longtime Toledo and Cleveland newspaperman who covered the waterfront, quite literally, distilled his long knowledge of the waterways into several volumes of Great Lakes shipping tales. He artfully filled the pages of *Ghost Ships of the Great Lakes* with sundry maritime mysteries, wrecks, disappearances, possible mutinies, and bad-luck superstitions. But, I complained silently, didn't the title promise *ghosts*? False advertising!

In truth, I learned, a "ghost ship" is not necessary a ship ghost.

The label "ghost ship" need not refer to a wrecked, sunken, dismantled, or otherwise defunct ship that somehow returns from a theoretical, scientifically unproven afterlife-realm and re-materializes. A ghost ship can also designate a boat that just sinks or disappears with no survivors, little if any wreckage or bodies, and is never pinpointed again by salvagers or divers. "She sailed into a crack in the lake and just disappeared" is a catchphrase on the Great Lakes to sum up the syndrome.

Still, there are Great Lakes ghost ships that seem to straddle both definitions. They were wiped from the waves in mysterious circumstances, with no survivors to explain, and the timeline of their final courses a confusion of contradictory sightings by other sailors and lighthouse-keepers. Did they see the doomed vessel itself – or its immediate ghost?

Norwegian author, sailor and master storyteller Peter Freuchen wrote this in *Peter Freuchen's Book of the Seven Seas*:

> Ships as well as men become ghosts, and that is because the ships have personality, as every sailor knows. This is why no seaman speaks of a vessel as "it." The spirit which animates the craft has been breathed into the wood, metal and rope sometime after they were put together in the shipyard. Sometimes the spirit is malign. Sailors always tell one story at least of such a perverse craft which seems to delight in maiming and killing.
>
> But mostly the personalities of ships are benign. They watch over the welfare of the men on board, so that even sailors who lived through the hard days of uncomfortable quarters and bad food felt an affection for the ships on which they served...

It is a wispish trace of eons-old maritime superstition, said to go back all the way to the Phoenician and Greco-Roman sailors of antiquity. That by designating their ships with feminine names and personalities, the ancient seamen could curry favor with gods of the ocean, Neptune and Poseidon. Ships were virtual "brides" of the male marine deities, who would then grant the ships and their crew protection and safety. Thus did ships become living beings, entities with spirits.

Folklore and tall tales, ancient and modern, speak of ghost trains, ghost cars, ghost planes – in a part of Wisconsin, ghost snowmobiles – and even houses and villages that manifest themselves as phantoms. In animist thinking, still prevalent in modern Asia, all manner of tools and objects harbor spirits. But in western mythmaking and lore, "ghost ships" are perhaps the most celebrated and romantic idea of an inanimate artifact that lingers in spirit form.

Many of these ghost-ship accounts, it would seem, serve to commemorate the memory of a lost ship still esteemed by sentimental mortals, such as the *Griffin* (see Chapter 1) or the *Edmund Fitzgerald* (see Chapter 4). Yet, if that were truly the case, where are ghost-ship reports of the *Titanic*? The *Lusitania*? The *Andrea Doria*? The USS *Arizona*? There seems something more at work than mere popularity that determines whether or not a ship becomes a "ghost."

On the open oceans, fleets of ghost ships have breasted the waves, from the *Flying Dutchman* to...the "Phantom Ship of the Bay of Chaleur." This latter is a celebrated apparition of a seemingly large, but hazily indistinct sailing ship, spotted in the Atlantic between Quebec and New Brunswick. The Phantom Ship of the Bay of Chaleur has been vouched for by Catherine Jolicoeur, a compiler of phantom-ship traditions, as something genuine, seen by trustworthy individuals – whether it was a recurring mirage, optical illusion or...something else.

The Canadian writer John Robert Columbo, perhaps in a whimsical mien, but certainly in a dictionary-literal one, has differentiated between two distinct species of undead ships. The rare "spectral ship" is one that glows, or even appears to observers simply as flames or luminescence. In 1876, the steamer *Sinclair*, carrying passengers and freight, caught fire and burned on Lake Superior, off 14-Mile Point within sight of the Ontonagon Lighthouse, with the loss of nearly everyone aboard. On the anniversary of the catastrophe – July 8 – it is said that the flames reappear, just northeast of the light, if the weather is good.

A "phantom ship" is the usual variety – if such a thing can be said to be usual. It is a ghost vessel that appears to observers to be solid, or, possibly, transparent. It may look in prime condition, but of clearly older, outmoded design. Or it may look tattered, rusted, and forlorn.

Bannockburn

For Dwight Boyer, and for many other storytellers, the archetypal Great Lakes ghost ship, defined as both vanished without a trace and supernaturally resurrected, was (or is) the *Bannockburn*.

She was a 245-foot Canadian steamer built in Middlesborough, Scotland in 1893. She undertook a transatlantic crossing and passage through the Welland Canal to serve as a "canaller" lakeboat for the Montreal Transportation Company. Receiving the highest rating by Lloyd's of London, she worked tumultuous Lake Superior safely for years. Then, in November, 1902, after taking on a heavy load of Canadian wheat at Port Arthur, Thunder Bay, she grounded in the harbor. An immediate safety inspection cleared her to move on her planned course, bound for the Sault St. Marie locks and Midland, Ontario, in Georgian Bay.

Besides the possibility that something dire was overlooked during the safety check, it may have been a portent of trouble that most of her crew were literally teenagers, hired on for less pay than more experienced sailors, although Captain George R. Wood was 37. In any case, in the late afternoon of November 21, the *Bannockburn* was sighted by Captain James McMaugh, of the steamer *Algonquin*, plowing through the choppy waves and visual haze of a rising gale, about fifty miles southeast of Passage Island.

Legend holds that Captain McMaugh simply turned his head to mention the *Bannockburn*'s progress to his first mate. When he looked back again, all 1,620 tons of her, the 85,000 bushels of grain, and the 20 crew – had vanished. Captain McMaugh concluded she had simply been lost to sight in the poor visual conditions. But the *Bannockburn* was gone, as though swept from the face of Superior.

Another steamer, the *John D. Rockefeller*, reported sighting a debris-field floating in mid-Lake Superior on November 25, but, unaware of the search underway for the missing *Bannockburn*, did not bother to investigate further.

Confusing reports came from a passenger steamer's night watchman that he had seen the lights of the *Bannockburn* that stormy night, or that she was aground near Michipicoten Island, or that she had found shelter near Slate Island. Captain McMaugh was even accused of mistaking another vessel for the *Bannockburn*, but he insisted on his identification. He theorized that an apocalyptic boiler explosion could have caused her complete destruction and sinking – somehow in less time than it took for him to turn and speak to his second-in-command and look back.

Only one cork life preserver was found that could be traced to the *Bannockburn* – and this could have washed overboard previous to ship's vanishing act. Divers and salvage teams have never found the wreck. Rumors stated that an oar with "B-A-N-N-O-C-K-B-U-R-N" cut into it as a final message was found by a hunter on the south shore of Lake Superior months later, but this seems more legend than fact, especially because, in some versions of the yarn, the letters were filled with human blood! A more solid remnant of the ship emerged in the winter of 1902-1903, when the Canadian lock at Sault Ste. Marie was drained for the off-season. At the bottom was found a steel plate from the missing freighter's hull, but how long it had been there was impossible to determine. Did this mean that the *Bannockburn* had severely lost her structural integrity?

Whatever happened, not long afterward – we are told – the phantom of the *Bannockburn* began to appear on Lake Superior, as though searching forever for safe harbor. However, exact details of the eyewitness accounts are nearly nonexistent. They seem more of an epilogue to the classic account of a vast boat that "sailed into a crack in the lake and disappeared."

Yet, if I were some kind of ghost-census agent, then from the extremely informal surveys I have taken of ghost-ship lore on the Five Sisters, the phantom boat that seems to have been the busiest over the years since her demise is not the *Bannockburn*. I would suggest to the harbormasters that the honor go to the holiday-bound *Rouse Simmons*.

Rouse Simmons

Lost the same year of the *Titanic* disaster, the *Rouse Simmons* has her name enshrined in the annals as "the Christmas Tree Ship." The *Rouse Simmons* was actually one of a number of schooners, dedicated to miscellaneous odd jobs and cargo-loading chores, operated by the Scheunemann family, originally northern Wisconsin settlers who relocated to Chicago. A three-master schooner, the *Rouse Simmons* had been built in 1868 and, in fact, was named after Rouse Simmons (1832-1897), a leading member of the Kenosha business community whose family enterprises of furniture and bedding would evolve into the Simmons Mattress Company. The 123-foot schooner hauled lumber between various ports for most of her career, that lumber later to include Christmas trees.

Even at the height of her fame, few Chicagoans ever knew the *Rouse Simmons* true name; she was just "the Christmas Tree Ship." But that same phrase could fit many vessels in the late 19th century that earned a trade ferrying a seasonal cargo of fir trees, mostly harvested from coastal Lake Superior and northern Lake Michigan. The trees were generally hauled to Chicago and Milwaukee for the benefit of thousands of German-immigrant families, who had brought the tradition of indoor Christmas trees with them from the Old World.

Because of the late-November season for the Christmas tree trade, the cumbersome heft of the cargo, and the tendency by the fir-tree harvesters to use antiquated, ill-maintained craft, Christmas tree ships often ran into trouble. These mishaps were bemoaned by the shipping-business press.

However, in the famously sentimental Chicago press of the era, the type of journalism burlesqued (barely) by Ben Hecht and Charles MacArthur in the play *The Front Page*, the Scheunemann's Christmas tree fleet became iconic of the season. The two Scheunemann brothers, August and Herman, were among the first to enter the Christmas-tree market, and August in particular was dubbed "Captain Santa" by eminent local newsman Vincent Starrett. In an era when Clement Moore's "A Visit From St. Nicholas" was newly minted, and even "Wizard of Oz" creator L. Frank Baum had offered his avid readership a fresh spin on the character in his *Life and Adventures of Santa Claus*, Christmas Tree Ships were the closest thing metropolitan dwellers could behold to genuine flying reindeer. Though not Father Christmas lookalikes – the dashing Schuenemann men favored fanned Kaiser Wilhelm mustaches more so than beards – they were known for their generosity, selling trees at resonable rates at 75 cents to a dollar, and giving away an occasional free one to the disadvantaged.

But positive media spin did not inoculate their business against the hazards of running aged, ailing boats months after the normal shipping season on the Great Lakes. August drowned in December, 1898, when a fir-laden schooner under his command sank within sight of Chicago.

Herman continued as a Christmas tree ship captain, bringing a schooner laden with firs to anchor every year at the Clark Street Bridge, his boat strung with electric lights illuminating a sign "CHRISTMAS TREE SHIP MY PRICES ARE THE LOWEST." If a family could not afford a tree, Herman was known to allow their children to do minor chores aboard the ship to earn one. Members of the city's homeless would be temporarily put to work in the unloading and distribution. The Scheunemann Christmas Tree Ship, still under full sail in an age of diesel and coal, was a Windy City institution. The fact that there were actually a series of successor ships did not matter.

Herman Scheunemann bought the *Rouse Simmons* in 1910. Her career had not been devoid of earlier tragedy. One deckhand fell fatally from her topmast, a second drowned overboard, and a third was crushed against the hull of another vessel brushing past. An alcoholic previous skipper, after his firing, committed suicide by morphine in a Chicago hotel. In retrospect, there has been much gossip about the crewman experiencing feelings of foreboding and bad portents – such as rats leaving the ship in droves prior to the final voyage.

Captain Scheunemann was one of the seventeen men aboard the *Rouse Simmons* on November 23, when a storm struck the ship off Wisconsin. She had come to Manistique, Michigan, and taken on some extra crew in addition to her inevitable stock of fir trees bristling the deck. It was an intended final run of the season. The next day she was seen in a blizzard off Kewaunee, Wisconsin, flying her distress flags. Rescue personnel caught sight of the stricken schooner and tried to approach the *Rouse Simmons* in a surfboat, but to no avail, and the old sailing ship vanished from visual contact.

The ship failed to make port, but the cargo of would-be Christmas trees started tumbling ashore in poignant heaps over the next week. It took some time for the finality of the loss to hit home, Barbara Scheunemann sustaining hope even as the schooner remained absent, day after agonizing day. In Chicago, the fate of the "Santa Claus Ship" made front-page news, the beautiful Scheunmann widow Barbara and angelic daughters figuring prominently in the coverage. Ben Hecht lent his literary talents to an ode that December:

> Roared the wind and rolled the wave
> That buried a helpless crew,
> And a Christmas ship in a Christmas grave
> Beneath the fathoms blue…

Despite their immense personal loss and the lack of the Christmas Tree Ship at her accustomed berth at the Clark Street Bridge, the Schuenemann women kept the tradition that Christmas by selling such wreaths and trees they could obtain throughout that December – some being evergreens received by railway, others the *Rouse Simmons* firs themselves, pulled up out of Lake Michigan. The women remained in the business and would continue holiday adornments as a Scheunemann family practice from a Chicago street-corner shop until 1933.

Weeks after the disappearance, the newspapers reported a message in a bottle, written and signed in Scheunemann's own hand, washed up on the beach off Sheboygan. It described two crewmen and a lifeboat being carried away in the teeth of the storm, and leaks overwhelming the schooner. "God help us," it concluded. What became of the note is unknown – as is a second bottle message, attributed to the other captain and business partner aboard, Charles Nelson, supposedly found in 1927, describing the ship about to submerge, all crew members tied together. While most stories about the *Rouse Simmons* mention the tragic missives, it is possible that both (or at least one) were hoaxes. Or not. It is true that, in 1924, Captain Scheunemann's own wallet was found intact.

The Christmas Schooner, a stage musical based on the *Rouse Simmons* has become an up-and-coming favorite with community theaters at the end of the year. Books, including a children's picture book, have commemorated the Scheunemanns. A white Zinfadel "Christmas Tree Ship" wine was bottled by the Von Stihl Winery in Algoma, Wisconsin, birthplace of Herman, and a spot in the harbor is Christmas Tree Ship Point. But of concern in the realm of ghosts and spirits, are the alleged sightings of the *Rouse Simmons* as a phantom.

The legends claim, naturally, that on Christmas Eve and Christmas Day, privileged onlookers can catch a glimpse of the old schooner still, though opinions disagree as to whether the phantom ship is more visible in dawn or at twilight. The November 23 date of her likely sinking also provides apt opportunities for viewing.

Tales of the *Rouse Simmons* as a phantom ship claim to date as far back as 1917, reporters speculating that some bizarre, but natural, phenomenon had stirred the Christmas Tree Ship up from her unspecified resting place on the bottom of Lake Michigan and sent her floating as a derelict (for what it's worth, divers found the shipwreck itself off Two Rivers Point, 180 feet down, in 1971).

Author Rochelle Pennington, writer of the definitive book on the Christmas Tree Ship, records that she personally met one eyewitness, a retired Sheboygan schoolteacher, Joyce Phippen, who testified to have beheld the *Rouse Simmons'* phantom on Lake Michigan on two occasions, many years before, from her stone cottage commanding an expansive view of the water. At one time, she said, the ship appeared out of the failing light of dusk. The second sighting, she said, came after dark, and in a misty-white haze the witness could make out ice and riggings. She told Pennington the vessel seemed "floating in air."

Various tale-mongering sources inform boat-watchers that the phantom is said to appear as a three-master, as tattered and ice-shrouded as she was when she succumbed to the great blizzard of 1912. Some storytellers specify that phantom fir trees are still lashed to her masts.

Those, at least, would give the *Rouse Simmons'* ghost the benefit of a positive ID, if the witness were keen-eyed enough. Otherwise, unless a theoretical ghost ship has the unmistakable profile of the *Edmund Fitzgerald*, it might go seen, but remain nameless.

Other Sightings

A much-read essay about a sighting of a phantom ship was published by Canadian artist/historian Rowley Murphy, and the evocative description crosses the line from mere believe-it-or-not to poetic literature. It tends to substantiate the claim rather than detract, that Murphy could not or did not attempt to identify the apparition he thought he saw in August, 1910, during a pleasure cruise on western Lake Ontario.

Along with his father, a cousin, and two other boats of pleasure-cruisers, Murphy found himself awakened at 1:30 a.m. by repeated whistle-alarm blasts from an unidentified steamer. By the moonlight, they saw a small steamship of slightly older design, about a half-mile off Etobikoke Creek. Her illumination had the quality of whale oil rather than electric filaments. Her distress signals continued sounding, so the men set out for the ship:

> As the boys in the dinghy reached the area where something definite should have been seen, there was nothing there beyond the clear and powerful moonlight, a few gulls wakened from sleep...but something else impossible to ignore. This was a succession of long, curving ripples in a more or less circular pattern, which just might have been the last appearance of those caused by the foundering of a steamer many years before, on a night of similar beauty... Something that had occurred in the more or less distant past, and which had returned to the consciences of living men after a long absence.

Another out-of-time steamship was sighted on at least two occasions (once in 1977) working her way up the Lester River in Minnesota, a traditional route for ships at the port city of Duluth to enter and exit Lake Superior. A Michigan schoolteacher logged a sighting of a two-masted schooner in July, 1966, in broad daylight off Ontonagon, Michigan, when nothing of the sort was known to be in the vicinity.

Among the lore of the treacherous Porte des Mortes, linking Lake Michigan to Green Bay, is that in 1940 four people on a small cruiser near Gills Rock spotted an old-fashioned schooner rigged with lights in the distance, a phantom that disappeared from view after the next cresting wave. This, by the way, happened under a full moon.

Anywhere between 300 and 400 shipwrecks have occurred in heavily traveled lanes off the largest lake island in the world, Manitoulin Island in Lake Huron. There, an unnamed spectral ship or "burning boat" regularly appears near Providence Bay, at the 3 a.m. hour on a night with a full moon. For best viewing, one is advised to stand where an old lighthouse guarded the rocky shore. Here, it is said, groups of up to 40 people at one time have watched what seems to the eye to be the outline of a schooner ablaze in the distance.

Niagara-on-the-Lake is a Lake Ontario community whose strategic location as several battlegrounds in the War of 1812 have left forts, battlefields, and rumors of the slain persisting beyond death – to the extent that those who do accountings of such things call Niagara-on-the-Lake the most haunted spot on the Great Lakes. Unsurprisingly, Niagara-on-the-Lake has a resident ghost ship. She is a small, single-master of archaic design and shows great wear and age as she materializes and then vanishes, at one point observed to leave a wake of fog behind her.

Unlike most of the Niagara-on-the-Lake spirits, often casualties of the clashes between American, British, and Indian-tribe armies, this phantom sailboat has no backstory to connect her to the War of 1812. A few authors have gone so far as to identify her as the *Foam*, a yacht assumed to have run across a shoal on windy July day in 1874; all seven men aboard, young members of the Royal Canadian Yacht Club, either drowned in the cabin or washed ashore on the beach of the New York side. But such connection is purely, necessarily speculative.

Other phantom ships, many returning to the visual universe supposedly as a mute warning of approaching storms or misfortune, include:

- On Lake Superior, the 310-foot, 2,392-ton iron ore steamer *Western Reserve*, rematerializing during the height of storms as the mighty ship that broke apart in a gale on August 30, 1892, leaving the wheelman the sole survivor;
- The 365-foot Canadian steamer *Altadoc*, wrecked (with no loss of life) on the Keweenaw Peninsula in a December snowstorm, 1927;
- The steamship *Hudson*, lost with all hands on September 16, 1901;
- The US Steel Corporation steamship *Lafayette*, grounded and sundered during an especially vicious late-November 1905 storm near Duluth;
- The tug *Lambton*, intended to service and provision Superior's many lighthouses, vanished with all twenty-two aboard in April, 1922;
- On Lake Huron, the *Hunter Savidge*, capsized on August 20, 1899, and that she was a 117-foot two-masted schooner would mean nothing to potential witnesses because her ghost manifests as she died – *upside-down*, just the hump of an overturned stern bobbing on the water;
- The decrepit, corpse-strewn 107-foot wooden barge *Joseph A. Hollon*, lost with four fatalities when the tug-boat tow-rope guiding her broke on the night before Halloween, 1870;

- On Lake Michigan, the *William H. Gilcher*, an iron-ore steamer that, at 318 feet long, was the largest boat ever built in Cleveland, but which vanished on October 28, 1892, later said to reappear when thick fog rolls in near Mackinac Island;
- The *Ella Ellenwood*, a 106-foot lumber-hauling schooner shattered (without human casualties) in a 1901 gale north of Milwaukee, at Fox Point;
- The steamer *St. Albins* was abandoned by her crew on January 30, 1881, when she seemed on the verge of sinking, yet she put in appearances in later years, smoke still uncurling from her stacks;
- On Lake Erie, the *South America*, a 100-ton, two-masted wooden schooner, disappeared with a cargo of salt in 1843;
- The *Marquette & Bessemer No. 2*, accorded the honor of "the *Flying Dutchman* of Lake Erie" for the way the 338-foot railcar ferry vanished without a trace east of Cleveland in a storm on December 7, 1909, amidst much bizarre confusion and the ominous discovery of a lifeboat full of silent, frozen crew corpses whose aspects suggested some sort of mutiny or struggle had occurred;
- On Lake Ontario, the aptly named *Ontario*, an ancient, 86-foot-long British sloop lost on an All Hallow's Eve gale in 1780, somewhere between Niagara and Oswego, is still visible on stormy autumn nights;
- Two undead schooners rumored to return on foggy nights, *Hamilton* and *Scourge*, were American sailing warships built for War of 1812, but the foe that sunk them was a sudden storm on August 8, 1813.

As to whether a ghost ship "normally" warns of bad luck or danger ahead, one might consider the legend of what a yachtsman reported from Point Aux Barques, which sits on the "thumb" of Michigan, on lower Lake Huron. Here, in the mid-1960s, during a foggy April, the witness saw what looked for all the world like an old United States Life Saving Service surfboat, with a ghostly crew of eight, appearing out of the mist and hailing the pleasure-boater, who had to steer sharply to avoid the bizarre vision. He could not make out what they were trying to tell him or remember positively the writing on the boat, which disappeared back into the haze. Straightaway the witness realized that had he continued unswayed on his planned course, he might have gashed open his hull on a reef.

And indeed, history records an entire United States Life Saving Service rescue team drowning with their vessel in another April, nearly a century before.

Lighthouses

After ships, it seems the most ghost-haunted constructions on the Great Lakes are, inevitably, lighthouses. Whole volumes have been written about haunted lighthouses throughout the world. There is a persistent folk-superstition that water serves to somehow trap spirits in place, to the point that when a person dies in a house, all containers of water – every vase, every pitcher – should be drained to prevent a haunting. And lighthouses have an abundance of water, within and without.

But there is more to these particular structures. A romantic notion of the isolation, the duty required by the lightkeepers who manned these sentinel beacons, some at a forlorn distance from the nearest populous area, has served to nurture the idea of ghosts here. That out of loyalty (or even loathing) for their profession, the inmates of the light cannot, or will not, leave – not even after death.

And there may *still* be more to it than that, as many old lighthouses, their days as vital beacons on busy waterways long over, are now administered as historic sites and publicly supported museums. It is not out of the question that the not-for-profit committees who administer them will happily foster the idea of a lingering ghost or two. It is said to be an attention-getter and an incentive for added visitor donations.

One Great Lakes historian with a fondness for ghost stories remarked that with every lighthouse he visited, if he were to inquire deeply enough among the staff, someone would finally admit to things happening on the site that could not be rationally explained. Ghosts? Opportunism? Imagination? Why not all three?

The Gibralter Point Lighthouse

It would be fitting that one of the oldest lighthouses on the Great Lakes also had a phantom or a poltergeist to go with it. The Gibralter Point Lighthouse was erected on Center Island in 1808, overlooking the Toronto region of Lake Ontario, as the second such Great Lakes beacon built (the first was erected at Niagara-on-the-Lake four years earlier). Its initial configuration was a fifty-two-foot stone tower (later increased to eighty-two feet) with a plain, non-revolving white lamp. By 1878, the metropolis around it had grown so much that the light was switched to green, to distinguish Gibralter Point from the surrounding urban illumination. In the 1950s, the light was extinguished for good, though the tower still stands as a significant Canadian historical site, tended by the Metro Toronto Parks Department.

If the ghost stories told are true, all this progress had a silent witness, the restless spirit of the first lighthouse keeper. His name was John Paul Rademuller, and he was a German immigrant who lived in a cabin (now vanished) next to the tower. In his downtime, so the tale goes, Rademuller maintained what we would now call a micro-brewery. And, it is said, that on January 2, 1815, he was attacked by three drunken guards from nearby Fort York, who coveted his homemade spirits. When Rademuller refused to serve them further, they attacked the keeper and chased him all the way up the spiral stairs of the lighthouse tower to the summit, knocked him senseless, then threw him over the edge to his death. As a grisly epilogue, the soldiers sought to cover up their crime by dismembering the body and burying the pieces in different places. In the twilight of the century, keeper Joe Durnan, in 1893, supposedly found scattered bits of human bones in the surrounding area.

Durnan said he could hear moans and see Rademuller's ghost, seeking the scattered mortal remains, on foggy nights. Known as "the Old Man" or "Old Man Muller," the ghost still ascended and descended the staircase to visit the beacon.

For what it's worth, in 1995, a Toronto guest-psychic visited the lighthouse at the behest of a kids' TV show taping a Halloween episode. Sensing numerous spirits from the get-go, she later stated that the legends have it all wrong: Rademuller was non-fatally roughed-up in a night of carousing with his drunken guests. Bloodied, dazed, and alone afterwards, he stole away from his ransacked post for good, effectively (perhaps unintentionally) faking his own murder.

The Seul Choix Point Lighthouse

Begun in 1892, the Seul Choix Point lighthouse overlooked a fishing community on Lake Michigan, guarding part of the Upper Peninsula so named by early French trappers because it was the "*seul choix*," or "only choice" accessible to land on the shore for some 100 miles. It was similarly the only choice for locating the 80-foot tower attached to the red brick keeper's house. Construction was completed in 1895, and while most other lighthouses throughout the Five Sisters have been rendered obsolete by automated antenna-like towers, this light still shines as the only lighthouse-navigational aid on the northern shores of Lake Michigan that remains fully functional as it was in its heyday. While a "working" facility, the Seul Choix Point Light is a showcase historical attraction maintained by the historical society of the nearby town of Gulliver.

The second keeper, in 1902, was Joseph Willie Townsend, an English transplant described as a heavy cigar smoker. He died in agony in August 1910, of some ailment now conjectured to be stomach cancer. His body was not taken to any accommodating funeral parlor but embalmed at Seul Choix Point, in the basement of the keeper's house, then brought up to the first floor, where the corpse lay in state for visiting relatives from Marquette.

In the 1970s, when Seul Choix Point functioned as a Coast Guard station, families of the Guardsman found table-settings suddenly altered, a phenomenon that continues to this day, with the table sometimes maneuvered to a different position when no one is looking. The charming explanation goes that William, having been born in Britain, takes umbrage to place settings in the kitchen in the American style, with the fork to the left of the plate. He will be correct as per British custom, with the fork on the plate, among other disruptions.

In 1988, renovation efforts at the keeper's house by inmates of the Camp Manistique Prison led to the structure's now well-established ghost tradition. Activity was associated with the recovery and restoration of a round table from the ersatz embalming-room basement, supposedly the only original piece of furniture left from the time of Townsend's demise. Members of the work team refused to enter an upstairs bedroom because of some nameless supernatural dread, claiming to hear disembodied footsteps and hammering. Furthermore they smelled cigar smoke without an evident source.

A technician installing a security system at Seul Choix Point, after inspecting the empty building, took fright at seeing an old man in a brass-buttoned lightkeeper's uniform staring down at him and his car from an upper window. Other visitors and several tour guides – sometimes simultaneously – have entered the bedroom to behold a man with bushy eyebrows, mustache, and beard, reflected in a sort of haze in the mirror. Two women have also been noticed occupying the mirror. Though Townsend has been duly enshrined as the uppermost ghost in residence, some have also claimed the old man in uniform to be a ship's captain who was visiting when he fell sick and died in the upstairs bedroom.

Big Bay Point Lighthouse

Big Bay Point Lighthouse, also overlooking Lake Superior on the sandstone cliffs of Big Bay Point, twenty-five miles northwest of Marquette, Michigan, has seen a second career as a bed-and-breakfast inn. Its principle ghost is usually said to be first of the keepers, William "Big Willie" Prior, described as a former military man who took charge of the light when it opened in 1896. He recruited his son, Edward, as an assistant. In 1901, however, Edward died of an infection from a leg injury suffered during his chores. Those who seek morals and messages in tragedy claim it was Big Willie's martinet insistence in not seeking a doctor and expecting that the wound would heal untreated that hastened Edward's death at 20. A few weeks later, the bereaved father disappeared. Ultimately, his decomposed remains were found in woods a mile and half away, where Big Willie had evidently hung himself. So goes the story.

The lighthouse was decommissioned in 1941. Beginning with a 1961 auction sale, the Big Bay Point light and keeper's quarters went through a succession of private owners, including two separate couples who maintained the complex as a B&B. Ghostly manifestations began to be reported in 1986, when owner Norman Gotschall first heard inexplicable banging noises. A cleaning woman took fright at a mystery man seen in a shower stall. Others reported the faint specter of a figure in the uniform of a lighthouse keeper, or a man in a military uniform with bright gold buttons, standing at the foot of the bed.

In 1990, the Gotschalls sold to a trio of Chicagoans, including another husband and wife, Linda and Jeff Gamble. They received consultations from at least three so-called "psychics" who informed them that, aside from Big Willie, the Big Bay Point lighthouse had other resident ghosts in addition to the keeper, especially a young woman from the 1950s, murdered on the site and unhappy that her fate had been forgotten. Depending on how much stock one puts into psychics, this may or may not have been an imperfect recollection/confabulation of a 1951 homicide among military personnel at Big Bay Point that inspired the novel (and film) *Anatomy of a Murder*. At last report, according to Linda Gamble, anyway, the ghosts, however one tallied them, were lying low.

Two Harbors Lighthouse

Ghosts make good yarns for the guests – as do the rumors about another lighthouse-turned-B&B: the 1892 Two Harbors Lighthouse, in Two Harbors, Minnesota. Though administered by the Minnesota Historical Society, the facility also hosts overnight guests. A handful of staff and visitors have noted noises in the building (especially from the kitchen), a locked armoire that insists on unlocking itself, and other oddities. For some reason, the nocturnal noises –

heard by one overnighter, but not others, in the same vicinity at the same time – were most prominent at 3:45 a.m.

The Presque Isle Lighthouses

On Lake Huron two lighthouses near Alpena, Michigan, share similar names and otherworldly traditions. The Presque Isle Old Lighthouse, only thirty feet tall, illumed with burning whale oil when the lantern first came to life in September, 1840. After the successor Presque Isle New Lighthouse went operational in 1870, the obsolete older lighthouse sat abandoned for some years before being auctioned to a local family, the Stebbinses, who proved to be lighthouse enthusiasts. Generations of the family gradually restored the relic, ultimately turning it into a unique museum and a site listed on the National Register of Historic Places. In modern times, a now-famous ghost story has lingered at the structure.

A retired couple named George and Lorraine Parris were hired as caretakers in the mid-1970s. In the summer of 1979, somehow, the lamp was accidentally left on again one night – human error rather than ghostly meddling. This was highly illegal, as the errant beacon could have caused a navigational pileup, and the Coast Guard removed the wiring and the gear mechanism to ensure the accident could not happen again. Yet, in May 1992, months after George Parris died of a heart attack, Lorraine Parris started seeing a glow in the tower (where the antique Fresnel lens had been permitted to remain). She rounded up friends and family who confirmed the phenomenon and ruled out reflections from car headlights or the floodlights shining on the building after dark. Lorraine Parris' young grandson had an explanation: "That's grandpa!" Through binoculars, witnesses also seemed to see a shadowy figure moving in the lamp room of the locked and empty lighthouse.

Subsequently, there were attempts to extinguish the glow by hanging heavy curtains and tarps, even removing light bulbs and changing the focus of the Fresnel lens. Yet witnesses still insisted they could see a luminescence. Some also reported hearing footsteps and experiencing strange feelings of dread. A little girl reportedly went up alone to the tower and then came down saying she had been speaking to a man in the lamp room. She identified him from a photograph – the late George Parris. Some others have theorized that the ghost is one of the original keepers. In the mid-1990s, the Stebbins family sold the lighthouse and museum to the township.

Alpena's Presque Isle New Lighthouse was built in 1870. In contrast to the stubby Presque Isle Old Lighthouse, this beacon's 113-foot tower, a narrow 19 feet in diameter at the base, with 144 steps ascending to the lens, is the tallest of all lighthouse towers on the Great Lakes. The tale most often told here regards a lighthouse keeper's wife who went insane because of loneliness and her husband's infidelities. Allegedly, he imprisoned her in a cell or tunnel beneath the complex, or perhaps inside that looming tower itself. Ultimately, he murdered her, and her vengeful shrieks may be heard carried by the wind on tempest-tossed nights. The lighthouse is now maintained by the Presque Isle Lighthouse Historical Society, and, open to the public, gives visitors a panoramic vista of Lake Huron.

The Pottawatomie Lighthouse

Rock Island State Park in Door County, on Lake Michigan, contains the oldest lighthouse in Wisconsin, the Pottawatomie Lighthouse. The thirty-foot house and tower was finished in 1834 with an oil-burning lantern. Local legends claim that ghosts abound at a nearby cemetery (especially phantom children), and that the Pottawatomie Light is haunted by the spirit of a keeper who committed suicide out of remorse when a fatal shipwreck occurred during his watch. Not long ago, two paranormal-inclined authors, Chad Lewis and Terry Fisk, fact-checked the yarns and found no such tragedy had ever happened, though three people did die in a 1902 shipwreck. During their perambulations, Lewis and Fisk heard noises sounding like slamming doors coming from the lighthouse – which was closed to the public and boarded up.

The investigators did determine that the first keeper, David E. Corbin, a War of 1812 veteran, suffered pangs of loneliness at his outpost. In 1845, he received special permission to take twenty days' leave to meet and marry a wife to bring back with him. In this mission, he was unsuccessful, and he died seven years later. The phantom children Lewis and Fisk did not perceive, even after a night's vigil camping by the cemetery.

Fairport Harbor Old Main Lighthouse

One should always remember in matters of ghost and spirit legends that, despite a proliferation of mostly laughable "reality TV" programs of young para-scientists stumbling around ruins with their infrared cameras and gadgets, pretending awe and surprise at every filmed dust-mote and lens flare – that anything resembling concrete "proof" of afterlife hauntings remains as elusive as Rowley Murphy's vanishing steamship on placid Lake Ontario. Perhaps the nearest thing to confirmation can be boasted by those around the Fairport Harbor Old Main Lighthouse on Lake Erie.

Located east of Cleveland, Fairport Harbor's seventy-foot beacon was opened in 1871, but made obsolete in 1925 by a nearby breakwater lighthouse. The old, conical light tower and its keeper's house, have since been added to the National Register of Historic Places and managed by the Fairport Harbor Historical Society as a maritime museum.

Allegedly, the former curator of the museum, who lived for a time inside the building, would glimpse a cat running around the place. She owned no cat, nor did she allow a stray inside, but nonetheless had an impression of a feline skittering about, to the point that she would amuse the elusive cat by making a toy out of a rolled-up sock, throwing it, and watch the shadowy form chase after it. She also claimed to feel an invisible cat jump in bed with her at night. Although there were rumors that the long-ago son of a lighthouse keeper died of smallpox and haunted the building, the ghostly rumors centered on the phantom cat.

In 2001, contractors were installing a new ventilation system for air conditioning in a crawlspace beneath the lighthouse. One workman, crawling through the dust, literally found himself face-to-face with the desiccated body of a cat – eyeless and mummified. The little carcass was recovered from its hiding place and left propped up by the stairs for the museum's publicist to find. Later, she would say, she screamed at first sight of it. The discovery made the local news media, and it would not be much of an overstatement that the preserved feline corpse became the most famous dead cat in Ohio – although, of course, there is no proof that this one provided the "spirit" that allegedly scampered through the lighthouse-museum. Fairport Harbor is home to an uncommon number of cats, as well as a local pet-products business. Either way, the mummy cat went on public display under glass for a time, among the museum's other relics and treasures.

One occult specialist noted an ancient practice of ritually sealing up an animal in the masonry of a building for luck (though coins are sometimes a more humane substitution); she wondered if this superstition might possibly have prevailed during the construction of the Fairport Harbor Old Main Lighthouse, in a community largely consisting of Old World seafarers of Finnish descent.

One of the Great Lakes' many so-called haunted lighthouses overlooks Lake Erie in Fairport Harbor, Ohio.

Neither Ship nor Lighthouse

Seaweed Charlie

There are a certain number of Great Lakes ghosts not connected with either ship or lighthouse. They just seem fond of the water. Perhaps the best known, at least in the Chicago vicinity, goes by the name "Seaweed Charlie." He is an apparition reported on the north shore of Chicago, where the city borders Evanston.

According to author Ursula Bielski, this ghost was a sight witnessed by thousands of well-to-do Chicagoans up until 1960 or so. Oblivious motorists passing by Calvary Cemetery on Sheridan Road would behold part or the whole of a perpetually replaying ectoplasmic drama. A young man would walk across the road from the Lake Michigan side, pacing back and forth at the locked cemetery gates. Only gradually did it dawn (or the legends take form) that the figure was deceased.

He is said to be the spirit of either a victim of a ship sinking or a plane crash. Some interpretations propose he was an anonymous student aviator during WWII, one of many neophyte pilots who practiced the dangerous skill of landing on top of a ship's deck in some converted carriers maintained by the US Navy on Lake Michigan for training purposes. Crashed into the lake and killed, his body never recovered, the aviator thus would rise from the waves that claimed him, stagger across the street and attempt to find rest inside the venerable cemetery, the oldest Catholic Diocese burial ground in Chicago.

…But his efforts were in vain, for the gates were always closed during his perambulations. Then, sometime around 1960, according to Bielski's version, the gates were one night accidentally left open. Thus the aviator's ghost finally found rest, and appeared to living eyes nevermore. Similar stories go so far as to put a name to the pilot: Laverne Nabours, who died in a 1951 crash during a training exercise at Glenview Naval Air Station.

Other sources say an apparition staggering across Sheridan Road to get to the cemetery has persisted well after 1960, and that some drivers fear that they have run down an errant jogger, only to find no one when they stop their vehicles and check. One of Chicago's top ghost-tour guides (hence, somewhat inclined toward the fantastic) collected a tale that, in 1993, two young ladies driving south on Sheridan Road perceived the car up ahead suddenly swerving to avoid someone. Then they saw what it was, a tall, thin glowing figure in an unseasonable long coat, crossing the road. When they spoke to friends about it, one girl learned her boyfriend's own mother had seen much the same phantom, many years before, in the same place.

While murky rumors link the lurching ghost with victims of the Chicago River *Eastland* disaster of 1915, or the earlier collision of the ships *Augusta* and *Lady Elgin* on Lake Michigan (see Chapter 4), author Leslie Rule, who has collected ghost traditions connected to violent crimes and unsolved murders, came up with a different conclusion. Her research proposes that the spirit is that of a Northwestern University freshman named Leighton Mount, who disappeared in the fall of 1921 during "rush week" at the campus.

Mount had left behind a lovelorn letter to a disinterested co-ed that some might interpret as a suicide note, and one of NU's star athletes told some friends he knew where the absent Leighton Mount was. Later, the Mount family received a telegram purporting to be from their son. But hopes for his return faded with a discovery made by a 12-year-old boy playing by Lake Street Pier in April, 1923. It was the bones of Leighton Mount, along with some decayed rope.

A murder inquest resulted, the prosecutor charging that fraternity brothers had tied Leighton Mount up at the Lake Michigan pier for an overnight-endurance ritual, alone all night, only to find him dead from exposure the next morning. Yet the trial ended inconclusively; Leslie Rule, for one, charging a cover-up by college authorities and influential families of the students involved. In a tale-teller's imagination, that provides more than enough reason for "Seaweed Charlie" to pace restlessly along Sheridan Road and at the gates of Calvary Cemetery.

For what it's worth, Dale Kaczmarek, president of the Chicago-based Ghost Research Society, spoke to the assistant sexton of Calvary Cemetery, who laughed and said that in all his years on the job, he had never heard of Seaweed Charlie.

Diana of the Dunes

South of Chicago, another ghost of the Lake Michigan beaches walks – or swims, or perhaps neither – at the Indiana Dunes State Park. There, folklore describes a vanishing woman walking or scurrying through the sands, furtively glimpsed by moonlight, or merely heard weeping. Unlike the most extreme tales of Seaweed Charlie, she has not been seen by thousands, which is fine concession to modesty. For this particular ghost is sometimes nude.

Cynical humorist and author Ambrose Bierce proposed that, logically, all ghosts should be naked – otherwise, clothing would have to have souls. Those who believe more soberly in spirits theorize that the apparitions of the dead will materialize in the way they imagine themselves – hence Seaweed Charlie and his coat, or Big Willie Prior and his uniform. In the case of the naked ghost of the Indiana Dunes, she may or may not wish to be seen that way; it is up to one's interpretation of the strange life and tragedy of Alice Mabel Gray, the woman they called "Diana of the Dunes."

Gray was born in 1881 to a working-class family (not, as would later be claimed by storytellers, a wealthy doctor's household). Intellectually gifted, she enrolled at the age of 16 at the University of Chicago and was an early woman graduate of that institution, earning a degree in Mathematics. She studied abroad in Gottingen, Germany, where she was strongly influenced by a European commune movement that discouraged material possessions and urged followers to return to the natural world. Upon returning to America, she worked in Washington, D.C. at the United States Naval Observatory and as secretary at a Chicago-based astronomy magazine, among other jobs that she seemed to find unfulfilling.

Later, the many legends told about Diana of the Dunes would claim a broken love affair sent her into self-exile, living like a hermit in the Indiana dunes. Another variation described a falling-out with her "aristocratic" family. In an interview with the Chicago press who were to make her famous, she told one reporter that she lost her job to failing eyesight, that working was "slavery," and she fled to the Indiana shoreline, east of Gary, in 1915. It was an area she loved and knew from childhood excursions and scientific dissertations and articles she had written.

Whatever the reason, Alice made a home in Ogden Dunes out of an abandoned fisherman's shack. She named it Driftwood. She hunted ducks for food, walked seven miles to the town of Porter for provisions and library books, sold game and berries to visitors, and generally lived off the land and her savings.

At this time in the press, especially the yellow journalism of the Hearst era, newspapers competed in the circulation wars by latching onto unusual human-interest fare – whether it existed or not. There was a vogue for sponsoring wilderness-survival stunts in some territories. Ex-Navy sailor Joseph Knowles, eventually to bear the brand-label nickname "Nature Man," was one such result. Knowles would be set loose in the Maine wilds, minimally provisioned (or clothed). How he set about fashioning his own buckskin leathers, building a shelter, and enduring the cold were breathlessly chronicled for readers by Boston and New England papers. Fakery and hype were frequent in these escapades, and rival newspapers took pleasure in revealing that Knowles had a pre-existing log cabin stocked with food all along.

One might well imagine the enthusiasm of the Chicago press to a revelation that a real "nature man" existed – and it was a woman, no less. A free-spirited Chicago maiden who had dropped out of society to dwell like a hermit on the Lake Michigan beaches.

…And swim in the surf. We are told that the first articles about Alice Mabel Gray hit newsstand-racks in 1916, thanks to complaints from the jealous wife of a fisherman. If the legend was to be believed, the angler had seen a beautiful mystery female bathing naked in the water, then dancing on the shores to dry herself. His spouse later lodged a complaint with the newspapers. It would not be too far a leap for the city desk to evoke the imagery famed in Maxfield Parrish paintings, depicting nubile beauties on a shore, under the stars. Thus, some bard of the Linotype machine tagged Alice Mabel Gray with the alliterative moniker "Diana of the Dunes" (a reference to the Roman goddess of the hunt) to put the gloss on rumors of a wild, beautiful hermit girl living in the wilderness of sand and reeds by herself and swimming nude in the surf. Copy compared her to a "milk white dolphin" or a "mermaid" or "nymph."

In truth, Alice Mabel Gray was small in stature, rather plain-looking by modern (and Maxfield Parrish) standards, more bohemian than glamorous. And Gray did not, in fact, live entirely alone. She is said to have had two different common-law husbands, though details are vague about the first. Nor was Diana of the Dunes entirely publicity-shy. She allowed two Chicago newspapers, the *Chicago Herald* and the *Examiner*, to print extracts from her "Dunes diaries." Excerpts from these journals do indeed read like melancholy missives to a faraway, inconstant lover. Alice identified him only by his first initial, "L," and hinted at his being a medical man of rising prominence – doubtlessly inspiring much reader speculation. In the company of reporters, she revisited Chicago in July, 1916, and was treated to her first motion picture. She argued for preservation of the Indiana dunes as a park, not developing it for factories. In 1917, during a "Great Dunes Pageant," she appeared as a special guest at the speaker podium at the Art Institute of Chicago to talk about conservation of the area's natural wonders. Other editorialists, who only saw the Dunes as real estate for manufacturing development, attacked her in print for her conservation sentiments.

Around 1920 or so, the slight Alice Gray took up with a six-foot carpenter, Paul George Eisenblatter, who used the name Paul Wilson – that, according to later reporters, was an alias to hide his past as an ex-convict. Some gave Wilson the nickname "Giant of the Dunes." The odd pair moved to a cottage called Wren's Nest at the western end of Ogden Dunes. Trouble followed "Paul Wilson" like a cloud, and he was accused of theft from neighbors and the June 1922 murder of a man whose corpse was found partially burned on the beach. Alice suffered a skull injury from which she never fully recovered, although the majority of accounts blame that wound not on Paul, but an overzealous local vigilante. This would-be avenger was Eugene Frank, a neighborhood-watch enthusiast and self-styled guide with a longstanding grudge against Paul. Alice and Paul went to confront him one June. What happened next was disputed in later testimony, as to whether Frank or Wilson attacked first. But Eugene Frank, backed up by his sons, shot the formidable Paul Wilson in the foot and smashed Alice in the head with his rifle-butt. Then the Frank men marched the couple to the local jail, two painful miles.

When Alice Mabel Gray died in the Indiana Dunes on February 11, 1925 (after marrying Paul in Knoxville, Tennessee, and briefly attempting to relocate with him to Texas), the initial verdict was uremic poisoning. But the autopsy verdict also showed internal damage to the abdomen. Later authors would call that consistent with repeated beatings and domestic abuse, presumably at the big fists of her "giant." At her memorial service Paul – in jail at the time of her passing – was said to have brandished a gun at reporters and relatives, and was arrested. Nobody today knows exactly where Alice is buried – only that it is somewhere in Oak Lawn Cemetery in Gary. Wilson did not have the money to honor her last request of cremation and a spreading of her ashes over the Dunes.

Her memory persists, however, as both a heroine of "Hoosier folklore," either still sighted by lucky fishermen as a mermaid-like nude in the water, or a fetchingly sky-clad phantom running along the tideline. Origins of the ghost rumor may have arisen from yet another melodramatic newspaper article, this stating that heartbroken Paul was hallucinating visions of Diana dancing down Mount Tom, the Dunes bluff off of which she had wanted her ashes dispersed. The Indiana dunes were indeed made into a state park in 1923, a federal park in 1966. Regional festivals and a "Diana of the Dunes" beauty pageant, in addition to the ghost stories, keep her name alive locally.

Author Andrea Lankford, a former ranger and collector of unusual national-park tales, recently tried to pin down any detailed narrative eyewitness sightings of Alice Mabel Gray returned from beyond the grave. Lankford could do no better than a wisp of a rumor that a park ranger saw someone or something assumed to be Diana of the Dunes in 1972. Janet Zenke Edwards, the first person to write a book-length biography of Alice Gray, concluded after a decade of research that there is no conclusive proof of domestic abuse in the relationship with the formidable Wilson. Claims that Diana of the Dunes had two children, by Wilson and the other man, are oft reported and false, said Edwards.

Whether a ghostly Diana of the Dunes does indeed linger forever at the Indiana beaches she loved, or yarn-spinners saved a final, posthumous exaggeration for the scandalous woman, at least history does agree that there actually *was* an Alice Mabel Gray.

The White Lady

Investigators have not yet been able to put flesh on the legend of the "White Lady," another female specter said to stalk Durand Eastman Park, a public common in Monroe County, near Rochester, New York.

Late in the 19th century, so the stories go, the teenage daughter of a local woman – whose name is sometimes given as Elisse – disappeared after one of her daily strolls along the shore. The girl had earlier told her mother she had an ominous feeling about a male neighbor, a farmer. The grieving Elisse told police the man was doubtlessly guilty, of kidnapping, rape, and murder, but she could prove none of it, and no arrest was ever made. Elisse, after despairing days spent searching the marshes for her child's body accompanied by her two loyal dogs, finally hurled herself off a cliff into Lake Ontario. Later, her dogs died of heartbreak.

Ever since, so the tale continues, Durand Eastman Park is the domain of Elisse, as a bitter apparition known as the White Lady. Once again joined by her faithful hounds, she emerges from Durand Lake and patrols the area, especially on foggy autumn nights.

Because she lost her precious daughter to the violence and lust of men – and because she herself was abused by her husband – the White Lady is hostile to males. She will not hurt women; in fact, if any husband or boyfriend guilty of infidelity can be tricked into coming to Elisse' stalking-grounds in Durand Eastman Park's equivalent of Lovers Lane, then an angry White Lady will materialize and force him to confess his sins.

There are those who have searched through Rochester-area police archives for any logging of such a missing-persons case, suicide, or murder on the books, but to no avail. A roundish brick structure overlooking Lake Ontario is cited as the White Lady's "castle" – but it was actually a public lookout for civil defense purposes.

It may perhaps be more rewarding to search through the detailed compilations of folklorists. In Hispanic folk belief, worldwide, there is the concept of "la Llorona," a ghost archetype whose legend began in Spain and migrated across the Atlantic Ocean to become particularly prevalent in Mexico,

Is the White Lady of Durand Eastman Park actually a Hispanic immigrant – namely, a mournful element of folklore called la Llorona? *1898 Motograph Moving Picture Book.*

Latin America, and ethnic enclaves of the United States. Some scholars have cited a German parallel of the White Lady legend, "Die Wiesse Frau," while others propose possible antecedents of la Llorona in a pair of Aztec goddesses, Cihuacoatl and Coatlicue.

La Llorona, in the classic sense, is the ghost of a mother driven to drown her own illegitimate children in a prominent area river or a lake. Subsequently, her phantom – clad in white with long black hair and clawlike fingernails – returns to search for them, often weeping as she does. "Weeping Woman" or "Crying Woman" are alternate names. Permutations of la Llorona have pollinated across cultures to the extent that she is a mother killed with her children as their auto (or coach) plunged off a bridge, or a mother whose child wanders away and drowns by happenstance. In some tales, it is the child who is the ghost, a baby's bodiless cries heard in the darkness. At other times, the mother and infant (and, rarely, the father) all haunt the scene. Loss of a child's life, almost always in water, seems to be the hallmark of la Llorona.

If there ever was a genuine inspiration for la Llorona, she has been eclipsed in the mists of time – forgotten, yet paradoxically, commemorated countless times over.

Minnie Quay

Were it not for the proof that she did actually exist, one might conjecture that eastern Michigan's Minnie Quay might also be apocryphal, or one of the many faces of la Llorona. This somewhat baleful ghost haunts the tiny Lake Huron resort community of Forester, north of Port Sanilac, a former lumber boom town. Minnie Quay was the daughter of James Quay and his wife, Mary Ann, who had come to Forester from New England. Their house, with the year "1852" prominent, still stands.

The legend goes that Minnie Quay, at age 14 or 15, fell in love with a Great Lakes sailor. Minnie's parents disapproved and forbade her from seeing him again. In a much-retold refrain from a subsequent folk-song about the girl (see Afterword Part IV), Mary Ann Quay scolds Minnie, declaring she would rather see her own daughter dead than with such a man.

In the spring of 1876, the sailor and his ship (no names provided) both went down in a storm. On May 29, 1876, the heartbroken Minnie was left home alone in charge of her little brother, Charles. Instead, she walked to the end of Forester's main pier, waved casually to passersby – and drowned herself in Lake Huron. Her parents buried her in the Forester Cemetery on the north end of town. Minnie's tombstone still stands amidst the family plot in a local graveyard, and visitors are known to leave small gift-offerings (mostly coins) behind in tribute to the girl who will be a teenager forever.

Some aspects of the ghost stories, however, suggest that Minnie has a peculiar, if not downright sinister, way of repaying the favor. Though the original Forester pier no longer exists, its decaying pilings are still visible, and stories say that Minnie reappeared bobbing in the water, beckoning to young female witnesses. While some say Minnie waits in the water for her sailor's return, another interpretation given that she wishes others will join her in suicide-by-

Great-Lake. At least one girl is said to have indeed killed herself after a Minnie Quay sighting – though this motif recurs time and time again in ghost-folklore, that there is at least one latter-day victim, as a warning to others, perhaps.

Many followers who know of Minnie Quay's tragedy mainly via the traditional ballad "Minnie Quay," prefer a more gentler and lovelorn temperament for the spirit, who supposedly haunts, with less lethal intent, the Forester Inn and a local restaurant and campground.

Black Dog of Lake Erie

Origins cannot be proven for a different, death-dealing Great Lakes ghost, an apparition which is not human in more ways than one.

The "Black Dog of Lake Erie" was an omen of disaster from the Great Age of Sail if seen padding on deck or running up and down the ship's masts. The black dog was itself an unspecified ship's mascot, a Newfoundland hound unfortunate enough to tumble off the deck as the vessel made passage through the Welland Canal. None of the sailors on duty troubled themselves to try and retrieve the desperate animal from the waves, and the dog drowned. Subsequently, a gate of the canal lock seized up, and the crew strained to free the ship. When the gates finally opened, the Newfoundland's carcass was revealed, wedged in the mechanism – as though in retribution.

A Newfoundland, pictured here in a 19th-century engraving, is traditionally given as the pedigree of the Black Dog of Lake Erie.

Afterwards the drowned hound haunted the boat, its mournful howling frequently disturbing the sailors' rest. And the Black Dog of Lake Erie materialized on other doomed ships, sometimes only visible to those sailors gifted with "second sight."

Though the callous ship from which the Newfoundland originally fell in an unspecified year remains nameless in legends, a few known shipwrecks and mishaps are cited in connection with the roamings of the dreaded Black Dog. The schooner *Mary Jane*, built in 1862, was supposedly docked at Port Colbourne, Ontario, in late 1862, when dock workers beheld the Black Dog leaping from her deck. On November 19, a storm smashed the *Mary Jane* to bits near Port Rowan on Lake Erie.

In November, 1875, the schooner *Isaac G. Jenkins* was undertaking a typically hazardous late-season passage from Chicago to Oswego, New York. As the ship crossed Lake Erie, a drunken helmsman frantically babbled about seeing the mythic hound of ill fortune scramble out of the lake and walk around the ship's decks. The man caused such a commotion, he was put off the ship around Port Colbourne. Supposedly, as the *Jenkins* passed through the Welland Canal, the sailer ran from lock to lock, shouting from the shore to his erstwhile shipmates that they had to get off the boat if they wanted to live. But the *Jenkins* continued on. On the last day of November, in uncertain weather, the ship disappeared near Oswego, New York, leaving minimal wreckage and no sign of the nine men who were aboard.

The epilogue to the yarn states that a New York farmer saw a bedraggled black dog tiredly coming ashore that same night, then vanishing into the darkness. The captain of the *Jenkins* owned a black dog, a small one, and so that is what the poor creature might have been. *Maybe…*

A later fabled victim of the Black Dog was the cargo schooner *Thomas Hume*, bound on Lake Michigan for her home port of Muskegon in the spring of 1891 when she vanished with all aboard on May 21.

Why the Black Dog chose to roam outside its customary territory of Lake Erie and the Welland Canal is unknown – perhaps it had to address the fact that the age of sail was coming to an end, surpassed by the boats driven by coal and diesel. Aside from ballads by musicians paying tribute to the lore of the Five Sisters, little has been heard from the Black Dog of Lake Erie in modern times.

The *Erie Board of Trade*

No discussion of Great Lakes ghosts can be complete without the *Erie Board of Trade*. It is perhaps the most famous of all Great Lakes ghost stories, at least to yarn-spinners of yesteryear, with the qualifier that it is likely fiction, or, if truth, unrecognizably disguised.

The story of the *Erie Board of Trade* appeared in the *New York Sun* newspaper on August 20, 1883, and was subsequently reprinted in Great Lakes newspapers and, around the turn of the century, even issued as a tiny book or pamphlet form, as *A Lake Huron Ghost Story*.

The article framed the yarn as a conversation between old salts on the New York City waterfront. "I saw a ghost once. I saw it as plain as I ever saw anything," begins one, and he proceeds to tell of his arriving in Chicago via canal boat looking for work. By chance, he admired the clean, trim lines of the *Erie Board of Trade*, a handsome-looking three-master carrying grain and coal across the Great Lakes. Her proud skipper, his name given as Jack Caster, was suitably impressed and hired the narrator on, for $2.50 per day.

But Captain Caster was a stern taskmaster, and many of the crew (the narrator excepted) left the ship soon, rather than submit to his orders and demands. Thus, for the next voyage another fresh face came on board, a Scot with a mane of red hair. Suitably, he was named "Scotty" in the tale.

Captain Caster took an instant dislike to Scotty. After the *Erie Board of Trade* sailed from Buffalo with a load of coal bound for Milwaukee, the wind died down and the ship was moving slowly, drawn along mainly by river currents. Caster, frustrated and half-drunk, ordered Scotty up the main mast to the boatswain's chair to "scrape down the topmasts" – mere busy-work, rendered dangerous because the ropes were frayed. The captain demanded that the Scot obey. A rope indeed snapped, and Scotty fell to the starboard deck. Blood bubbling out of his mouth, he cursed the ship, the Captain, and the Captain's family with his dying breath.

At Cleveland some of the crew left, having had enough, but the rest stayed on. During the first night on Lake Huron, the narrator and Captain Caster saw a misty white shape rise from the starboard deck. In the twilight it resolved itself into a luminous apparition of Scotty, still uttering his curse, and the ghost stretched its arms to the two nearest masts and, like Samson in the Old Testament, began to literally tear the ship's sails apart. With this initial act of revenge, the ghost disappeared, and only quick thinking by a relief crew kept the *Erie Board of Trade* maneuverable. Soon she put into Chicago. There the narrator jumped ship – while he still could.

When Captain Caster and the *Erie Board of Trade* left Chicago, the ship, and all those remaining aboard her, disappeared somewhere on Lake Huron. In some embellishments of the original tale, the ship reappears on the water from time to time as a phantom herself.

The story of the *Erie Board of Trade* has become a classic of Great Lakes folklore. Lee Murdock, a popular Illinois-based singer of Great Lakes chanties and spook stories, recorded a ballad based on the story that gives the Scottish sailor the name "Red Monroe" (not to be confused with "Young Monroe," ill-fated protagonist of a traditional ballad of tragedy among Upper Michigan lumbermen).

There is only one problem – that in the carefully kept and maintained registries of shipping on Great Lakes in the 1800s, nobody has yet found any trace of a ship called the *Erie Board of Trade*. There was a *Chicago Board of Trade*, whose owners had something of a shady reputation for deliberately sinking the boat to reap an insurance payout. But the *Chicago Board of Trade* is known to have wrecked, for good, on rocks in Lake Erie in 1900, well after the newspaper account. And no record exists of a captain named Jack Caster, especially one who, in the story's dialogue, hails specifically from Milan, Ohio.

Newspaper journalists, even for mainstream "respectable" papers, right up into the early 20th century, were not above making up outlandish yarns to fill column inches or exercise their considerable imaginations. If the tale of the *Erie Board of Trade* is not a confabulation, it certainly does a marvelous impression of one.

Still, it will likely be repeated, with some permutations – most lately on the World Wide Web and multimedia listings of "true" ghost stories. Here, also, the Black Dog of Lake Erie roams from time to time, in electron seas.

When it comes to ghost stories, where the cut-and-paste of repetition, error, and deliberate exaggeration makes the old schoolyard game of "post office" seem like a model of accuracy by comparison, it seems often that the hardest ghosts to urge on their way into a life of peaceful repose in the next world are the ones who never existed.

A 2009 incarnation of the "Christmas Tree Ship" arrives to a musical serenade from Lake Erie into a landing on the Vermilion River.

The *Rouse Simmons* and the souls aboard may or may not have found a navigable passage back from death itself. But, in the final rolls, this vessel does enjoy the most enduring and munificent of possible afterlives. With the dawn of the 21st century, a new Great Lakes tradition around the holidays is to re-enact the landing of the Christmas Tree Ship. A stand-in for the Scheunemann schooner now arrives every winter in Chicago, dispensing fir trees and charitable gifts under the auspices of a Christmas Tree Ship Committee. Other Great Lakes port communities have begun to adopt the practice, usually employing a trusty – and very much alive – modern Coast Guard vessel. A ghost ship, as it were, of Christmases Past, Present, and Future.

GREAT LAKES
BREWING CO.

Lake Erie Monster
A Handcrafted Imperial India Pale Ale
Cleveland, Ohio

The nefarious Lake Erie Monster generously lent his/her likeness to a lager created by the Great Lakes Brewing Company, a Cleveland-based brewery known for its fine ales as well as sustainable practices and openness to monsters. Label design by Pat Wilkinson and Brittney Fuchs. *Courtesy of Great Lakes Brewing Co., Cleveland, OH.*

Monstrous Tales
or
How to Explain Your Dragon

In Which Mysterious Aquatic Wildlife of the Great Lakes Yet Unrecognized by Scientists and Fishing License Agencies are Enumerated and Described. Strange Sightings and Flagrant Hoaxings in the 1930s on Lake Ontario. Conspicuous Courage of a Harbor Official in Collaring a Supposed Sea Serpent with a Crowbar. A Possibly Playful Lake Erie Monster Acquires a Name (or Two, or Three) and a Recognition as a Marketable Monstrosity.

O nce, we took a trip away from the drab city where we lived on the south shore of Lake Erie and drove west, along the shoreline road, and pulled off impulsively to a private beach near the community of Huron, Ohio. A storm had recently passed, leaving the air cool but clear, and the moistened beach sand was dotted here and there with deposits of jetsam dredged from the lake bottom by the waves.

Among the dirt and weeds, at widely scattered intervals, lay small...creatures, dead. Saurian and snakelike they were, about a foot long and a few inches wide, with elongated bodies ending in a largely featureless head of the same width, and four rudimentary legs. We had never seen such animals before. And our fancy did take control of us. Had we made a momentous discovery? Had we found a larval form of the fabled *Lake Erie Monster*, an enigma sighted in this inland sea since the 1800s, when it sometimes bore the name "the Great Snake of Lake Erie?"

Yarns of mysterious, large freshwater creatures, unrecognized by science, swimming in lakes and rivers, exist parallel to the ocean's eons-old legends of "sea serpents." Lake monsters are usually said to be generally serpentine (though with fins or flippers), varying in size from eight feet to eighty. Some seem like marine dinosaurs of the Mesozoic or Jurassic, others more huge eels or magnified otters. When in motion, more often than not, they plow through the water with an undulating rhythm, not unlike a giant seal (through on rarer occasions the side-to-side choreography of a snake is reported). A very few witnesses glimpse the creatures lurching about on land. In some instances, whiskers, hair, and horns are perceived. Sometimes, so rumor asserted, their giant carcasses had become stranded, or a specimen – perhaps a smaller juvenile – had actually been captured in a fishing net. Then no more was heard from it; any trace of positive evidence vanished.

And so do "lake monsters" remain an unconfirmed claim, and perhaps unprovable myth, from the world-famous "Nessie," the elusive denizen of Loch Ness in northern Scotland, to "Champ," a long-necked creature said to dwell in Lake Champlain, which connects tenuously to the St. Lawrence River off the Great Lakes.

It is a provocative, but extremely farfetched premise, that unknown, exotic animals of amazing size and bulk may have gone undiscovered by modern zoologistists. Few serious researchers put credence in lake monsters, though a handful of scientists have gone so far as to give Latin-classification names to some such animals, in either full sincerity or purely whimsical moods. It was evidently in the latter demeanor that Ohio State University oceanographer and zoologist Charles Herbendorf suggested a Linnean scientific name for the Lake Erie Monster. He called it "Obscura eriensis huronii," or "rarely seen, indigenous to waters of Huron."

Had we in fact discovered an *Obsura eriensis huronii*? We put the small corpse into a plastic bag with a dousing of rubbing alcohol for preservation, and took it with us a few days later on a visit to the Cleveland Museum of Natural History. "Cryptozoology" is the name given to the para-science of unknown-animal hunting and research, and our career in the field as intrepid monster-seekers was short and unproductive; we were told by a Museum expert that what had washed upon the beach in Huron were common mud puppies, a salamander-like amphibian normally at home on the lake bottom. For reasons not quite understood, the species undergoes a "die-off" from time to time, and the one we had found had lost its recognizable exterior gills to decay, explaining our confusion. We left the little body unceremoniously in a trash bin outside the Museum and went on our way.

There is a quote from a disbelieving scientist in the Hollywood classic *The Beast From 20,000 Fathoms*, that "if all seamen's reports of seeing monsters were laid end to end they'd reach the moon." Those who look into such things, the so-called cryptozoologists, have remarked on a "monster belt" or "monster latitudes," corresponding roughly between 45 degrees and 60 degrees north latitude, where such phenomena seems most well-documented. Most of the Great Lakes fall within these "monster latitudes," and parts of them have developed monster traditions, as have other, smaller lakes connected through the maze of Canadian river systems. Some broad-minded scientists and the obsessed amateurs who comprise the field of cryptozoology have suggested a possible prehistoric holdover breeding throughout this lake and river network that could explain the sightings. This is the "zeuglodon," or *basilosaurus*, a mammalian ancestor of the modern whale, last known to have swum the seas about thirty-seven million years ago, in the Eocene. Zeuglodon fossils exhibit a streamlined elongated body, up to seventy-five feet in length, with a fearsome mouth of sharp teeth and a possible dorsal fin.

A vintage engraving depicting the long-necked plesiosaur and other seagoing dinosaurs from the Age of Reptiles, popularly cited as being today's water-monsters.

The long, bony, armor-plated sturgeon fish is a rather more probable suspect.

More skeptical opinions are that wandering seals find their way into freshwater communities from the ocean via the St. Lawrence River, and their unfamiliar presence triggers monster hysteria.

Lois Beardslee, an Ojibwe author, artist, and teacher, who has lived much of her life on Lake Superior (see Afterword, Part I), states that colonies of otters often play in rows, their slender bodies and tails synchronizing above and below the waterline in an uncanny replica of one single, sinuous animal. Another answer would be misidentification of now-rare freshwater lake sturgeon, a primitive fish, unchanged essentially since the Triassic Era, capable of living more than 120 years, yet poignantly fished to near extinction for its eggs, a gourmet delicacy. With bony plates along its back, the sturgeon may also be responsible for monster reports, although five or six feet in length are standard for the North American sturgeon. Saltwater and European sturgeon can be more than twice that size.

Yesteryear's newspaper lake-monster encounters – most particularly those describing fearsome giant serpents with polka dots, bloodshot cyclopean eyes, breathing fire and smoke – are certainly journalistic hoaxes, a pastime of the frontier press fitfully afflicted with a shortage of worthwhile news to print. Modern Internet rumors are even less trustworthy.

Yet to gaze upon the Great Lakes, an aquatic habitat vast enough that any single one of the Five Sisters could dwarf Loch Ness, there would indeed seem enough room for something gigantic to hide, whether in the imagination or in reality.

Indian legends speak of "monsters," as whites would call them, mostly in terms that personified storms, waves, or natural forces that could overtake men in their canoes. The Ojibwe described a tremendous sturgeon in Lake Superior, able to capsize and sink anything the tribes could float. Ojibwe and Potowami along the north shore of Superior believed in Mishi Bizhou (also known phonetically to the Europeans as "Mishipishu") a huge underwater lynx that violently stirred the waters with a great tail and could destroy entire villages. Another Lake Superior creature, Michigaamigag (or Mishi Ginabig) is depicted as more snakelike, and with antlers. Surviving petroglyphs of such entities stirred the imaginations of today's self-styled monster hunters, as the appearance of a serrated back and horned head suggest the popular notion of a dinosaur.

The oldest white-European Great Lakes monster reports hail from Lake Ontario. In July, 1817, crew of an unspecified vessel reported a huge, black, snakelike creature, about a foot in diameter and 30 to 40 feet in length, in the water three miles from the Canadian shoreline. A similar serpentine creature was sighted in the spring of 1821, on the St. Lawrence River swimming for Lake Ontario.

That summer the *Palladium*, a newspaper published in Oswego, New York, carried an account by the crew of a large, freight-hauling canoe that while they were 20 miles off shore, 100 miles east of Niagara, they beheld what looked like a "burnt log," 25 feet long and motionless on the surface. But it did not remain motionless for long. As the canoe approached within 60 feet, a tall, snakelike head and neck rose 10 feet out of the water, and a ferocious churning, presumably by the monster's tail, spouted water almost as high. The creature, estimated at 37 feet long 2 feet wide at the most visible part, propelled itself away, at a distance estimated of two miles. Then it turned back and seemed to make for the general vicinity of the canoe. The men loaded their guns, preparing to kill this huge serpent if possible, but before they could fire, the beast submerged and was not seen again. The scullers of the canoe pulled a "lively oar" to leave the area as quickly as they could.

Near the Niagara River, according to the August 5, 1829, *Farmer's Journal and Welland Canal*, children and adolescents had been playing on the lake shore, near the mouth of 10 Mile Creek, when suddenly "a hideous water snake, or serpent, of prodigious dimensions," appeared. It was about twenty to thirty feet long with a foot-wide head festooned with "warts" or "bunches." This apparition was a small fry compared with the large, snakelike creature reported in 1833 by the captain of the schooner *Polythermus*, in the water near the Duck Islands. Visible for about fifteen minutes on a June evening, passing unperturbed under the very stern of the ship, the immense blue-brown serpent, making an eastward course towards the St. Lawrence River, was estimated at 175 feet long – the most sizable Great Lakes monster logged yet to date. To put that in perspective, the blue whale, the largest known animal in human history, spans 100 feet.

According to the *Prince Edward Gazette* newspaper in 1842, two young brothers and a family friend armed with a rifle stalked a monster for some two miles off the shore, roughly from Gull Pond to the Point Petre lighthouse at the end of the Prince Edward Peninsula, at which point the unsuccessful hunting party lost the creature in deep water. It was described as up to forty feet long, with bright eyes rather like those of a horse, which seemed to blink in the sunlight.

Not far from the Prince Edward Peninsula, a series of inland-sea-monster sightings took place in the mid-1860s along the Bay of Quinte, entertaining readers of the Canadian newspapers while Civil War dispatches dominated the press to the south. In September, 1864, an especially aggressive creature with a bulldog-like head, uttering "a dreadful noise" supposedly hounded a reputable local man, Julius Baker and his wife, sending them rowing for the shoreline at Trenton. At times, the animal was said to have dared to approach up to a few feet.

An 1867 *Detroit Free Press* account described a Lake Michigan creature sighted by the crews of two ships and a fisherman; the monster, about twenty feet of which was visible, had whiskers or barbels on its snout, a serrated back, front flippers or legs, and a long, possibly hair-covered tail. Like the Bakers, the witnesses had the rare privilege of hearing this monster in addition to seeing it – a "half puffing like a heavy breath, and half an actual vocal sound, harsh and grating."

In August, 1867, crews of two boats, the *George W. Wood* and the *Sky Lark*, reported a serpentine creature off Evanston, Illinois. A fisherman named Joseph Muhlke later saw it a mile and a half off Chicago's Hyde Park.

Eastern Lake Ontario's creature surfaced again on September 14, 1881, within sight of the steamer *Gypsy*, on a run from Ottawa to Kingston, Ontario. The beast, appraised at a possible forty feet in length, apparently reacted to the ship's presence with great commotion in the water as it sped for the Rideau Canal – and those who put stock in water monsters have surmised that the noise-sensitive animals will, naturally, shy away from such engine-powered vessels and be less disturbed by masted sailing ships.

More sightings of Kingston's unusual denizen took place in 1882 and 1888. In time, the creature would come to gain an affectionate nickname: Kingstie. Encounters with Kingstie tend to have the flavor of fanciful newspaper hoaxes of the era, such as the 1892 allegation that a husband and wife in a skiff off Brakey's Bay were attacked by a monster serpent "with eyes like balls of fire," that the man repelled by a beating with his fishing pole.

During the first Great Depression, a populace weary of joblessness, plant closures, soup lines, Wall Street havoc, and empty promises of "prosperity right around the corner" sought diversion in the news headlines of the media "silly season," which, more often than not, it seemed, fell in August. Flagpole-sitters, grueling dance marathons, Ripley's Believe-It-Or-Not, swamis, magical beings in the form of talking mongooses – all those and more had their turn in the headlines or newsreels during the depths of the 1930s. But few captured the attention of readers worldwide as the 1933 sensation surrounding the so-called Loch Ness Monster of Scotland, which, decades later, remains stubbornly unproven.

But, on the Canadian shores of Lake Ontario, there was an immediate antecedent – the "summer of the sea serpent" in July and August of 1931, starting with a report that a thirty-foot long snakelike creature had been sighted in the water by campers at Lakeview Beach at Oshawa, east of Toronto. More witnesses came forward, some stating they had shot at the monster, with no visible effect. According to two physicians who, from their sailboat, beheld the creature in August, it was a thirty-foot monstrosity with but one eye in the middle of its forehead and antler-like horns. Two boys fishing off a pier west of Oshawa saw an even more extreme monster swimming in the lake on July 23, about 150 feet from shore. From their vantage point, they said, it appeared to have three heads.

An exceptional mass-sighting on August 1 at Port Credit beach, west of Toronto, drew the curtain, mostly, on the Summer of the Sea Serpent. Hundreds of Saturday bathers, including a swim team in training, glimpsed a monstrous creature in the water late in the day, and the word spread across the beach. At dusk, as the tale is dramatically told, the caretaker of Port Credit, one Ambrose Adams, rowed out to confront the unknown, armed with only a crowbar in case of trouble. Adams returned in the dark, telling the throng, plus a reporter on the scene, that he had captured the beast indeed and left it tied to the local lighthouse. The reporter sallied out to inspect the find via flashlight. Tied to the Port Credit lighthouse was a homemade monster created out of a length of seaweed with a rocking-chair horse at the fore.

In 1979, furthermore, a few local men stepped forward and claimed to have perpetrated Kingstie sightings of the 1930s, also with a mock lake monster created out of floating bottles in Cartwright Bay. Despite these crippling setbacks to the Kingstie legend, rumors of large, unknown animals in the area continue, albeit nothing on the level of 1931.

Sightings of unidentified residents in the other Great Lakes persisted into the 20th century. What was originally – shades of Kingstie – assumed to be a large, floating cask in the waters of Lake Michigan turned out to be the head of a great serpentine beast, that was seen off Milwaukee, then later in the Milwaukee River itself in the early 1900s. In Lake Huron's Georgian Bay, in 1948, more than a dozen people aboard the *City of Detroit III* saw a serpent estimated at sixty feet long – though newspaper descriptions specifying green and purple scales and fearsome horns smack of journalistic exaggeration. Seal-like animals swam near Wasaga Beach in 1938 and Kincardine in 1975.

Smaller Lake St. Clair harbored a snakelike monster blamed by one witness for dragging a fisherman's horse into the water (and presumably devouring the unfortunate equine) in 1897.

Hoaxes and frauds too are not unknown on these lakes. At the same rough time period as the Kingstie and Nessie sensations, in the early 1930s, after a number of monster sightings on Lake Michigan, what appeared to be a sham serpent made of thirty feet of wood and wire, was found washed ashore at Luddington, Michigan. Lake Superior's "Pressie" is a reputed gull- and deer-devouring monster of the Upper Peninsula of Michigan, about seventy-five feet in length with a whale-like tale, localized around the Presque Isle River, though the main Pressie evidence seems to rest on a few wispy anecdotes and a rather dubious photograph.

Still, Lake Erie's monster would seem to be the most noteworthy unknown beast of the Great Lakes, if only because of a veritable cottage industry spun off the traditions of a giant serpentine thing lurking in the shallowest of the Five Sisters.

Erie's creature was reportedly seen as early as 1793, by the sloop *Felicity*; its captain chanced to startle a giant serpent in the shallows of the Lake Erie Islands. An 1819 article by 19th-century science writer Constantine Samuel Rafinesque described a sighting (from two years earlier, July 3, 1817) of a freshwater "huge serpent." The Erie animal, witnessed by a schooner three miles out from shore, was between thirty-five and forty feet long, a foot in diameter, and dark brown or black. Rafinesque lamented that witnesses failed to say whether it had smooth skin or scales, and he surmised the animal to be a form of giant eel.

A restaurant in Huron, Ohio, pays tribute to "Lemmy," one of the town's famous adopted citizens.

The monster laid low for about a half century, and then in July 1873, there came a strange story. Railroad workers near Buffalo claim to have seen a twenty-foot-long creature with a toothy mouth disclosing a double-row of teeth. Furthermore, it spouted water skywards in the manner of a whale. When cattle began vanishing from the area, with incriminating tracks and marks leading to the water, a posse of armed monster-hunters in a chartered tugboat patrolled for the menace. Unlike future generations of dogged cryptozoologists, these hunters did indeed spot the marine marauder and fired their shotguns into the water, causing the horror of Lake Erie to howl and writhe before sinking away. So went the yarn, anyhow.

Next in the chronicles is a claim from yet another July, that on the 30th day of that month in 1880, the schooner *General Scott* sighted a forty-foot serpent about a foot in diameter that swam close to their ship off Erie, Pennsylvania, on a fine, calm day. It exhibited no hostile intent.

In May 1887, two brothers named Dusseau reported a large, fish-like animal, about twenty to thirty feet long, "with long arms which it threw wildly in the air," on a beach known as Locust Point, west of Port Clinton, Ohio. Apparently, in its death agonies, the creature suddenly lay still. The Dusseaus left to fetch a rope to haul their discovery in shore, but when they returned, the "fish" was gone, leaving only scales the size of silver-dollar coins.

An 1889 newspaper from Sandusky quoted fisherman as having seen the water monster at Kelleys Island. An 1892 report from Toledo claimed the captain and crew of the schooner *Madaline*, inbound from Buffalo, were amazed at a fifty-foot serpentine creature with fins, about four feet in circumference, violently churning the water "as if fighting with an unseen foe" before coming to rest and temporarily allowing the mariners a look.

"It was a terrible looking object. It had vicious, sparkling eyes and a large head." Fins were visible at the sides of the dark-brown body.

In October, 1894, a Baptist pastor from Silver Creek, New York, his wife, and another woman were considered unimpeachable witnesses to the appearance of a creature out on Lake Erie. The animal cruised at a rate of about ten knots, with a fifteen-foot neck and large head arching out of the water. Along the neck and back were a double-row of fins, about a foot apart, went the description.

Charles Herbendorf, mentioned earlier for playfully endowing the Lake Erie Monster with an official Latin name in the late 20th century, suggested that a reasonable explanation for monster sightings would be simply groups of fish, perhaps carp, gamboling together, likely compressed into a long, squirming single file by shallow sand bars. In fact, in May 1896, a quartet of onlookers at Crystal Beach, by Fort Erie in Ontario, thought they were seeing exactly that. But then the shape moved towards shore, and one of the witnesses, a woman, is recorded as saying "Why, it is all one fish!"

According to a ship captain named Beecher, one of the lucky four, the "fish" was a thirty-five-foot-long serpent with a dog-like head and eyes the size of silver dollars. It stayed in view for forty-five minutes as dusk settled on a peaceful lake. The creature moved slowly, occasionally rolling to show a light-colored underbelly or a humped back. Beecher seemed satisfied it had no flukes like a whale or porpoise or rear flippers like a seal, but rather a true reptile-like tail.

Captain Beecher threw stones at the monster, which would lunge at the projectiles as if they were prey, traveling its own length to try to catch them. As lake monster reports go, it is most charming and singular that one of these entities would play "fetch."

Later, a boy at Port Dover is recorded as having seen much the same creature, his family divulging from neighbors that they too had knowledge of the thirty-five-foot lake serpent, but had kept quiet about it for fear of ridicule. In the same fashion, a tugboat pursued a monstrous creature with a horse-like head off Long Point in the early 1900s, but it dove away and eluded them, the crew not speaking of the apparition for the next twenty years.

In 1931, there came an electrifying *Associated Press* bulletin, dateline Sandusky: Fisherman had stunned and hauled ashore a twenty-foot-long serpent with dark, alligator-like hide. Some cryptozoological books and websites still refer to this remarkable specimen, generally ignoring that the men turned out to be hucksters, connected with the carnival trade, who were trying to charge admission to locals to gawk at a python snake in a darkened tent as their "monster."

A community newspaper, the *Ottawa County Beacon*, tallied "modern" sightings of the Great Snake of Lake Erie beginning with reports from 1960 and 1969. The latter witness, at South Bass Island, said an underwater snake of indeterminate length and two feet in width, nosed up to within six feet of him. The monster re-emerged with spates of widely publicized sightings in the 1980s and '90s – ironically, a period when industrial pollution in the lake made its viability as a habitat for many fish a dubious proposition.

A frightened boater in 1985 called the Coast Guard to report the monster churning the water aft of him. A 1983 woman witness had a similar feeling of terror when what she thought was an upturned boat off Rye Beach in Huron, paddling along at 5 a.m. on a foggy morning, resolved itself to be a large, dark-green animal sporting a turtle-like back, a long neck, and prehistoric-looking head – with a curving jawline suggestive of a grotesque grin. She estimated it as about thirty-five feet long. And, she added, it smelled awful.

A folk-sculpture of the Lake Erie Monster in the Huron River.

Also in 1985, two Cleveland Coast Guardsman alleged a snakelike monster off a municipal beach. In 1990, two Huron firefighters – one a retired Coast Guardsman – spied the monster as a humped, thirty-five-foot-long shape, which they declared not to be a log or a sea wall. A couple running a charter-boat business saw something very similar at Kelleys Island. A few years later, at Huntington Beach, a popular suburban summer hangout west of Cleveland, a beachful of witnesses on a July evening saw a ridged back, estimated between twenty-five and fifty feet long, rise out of the water, not far from the shore. Allegedly, there were no boats nearby to create a freak wave effect.

In that last case, I had the opportunity to speak personally with one of the eyewitnesses, who had been visiting the beach that day with his cousins. He said that, afterwards, they paged through volumes of animal life and decided that what they beheld at Huntington Beach most nearly resembled a sturgeon fish, enormously magnified.

"I was a little afraid to go in the water after that," he told me.

Most Lake Erie Monster reports focus on the southwestern part of Lake Erie, along the Ohio coast the Lake Erie Islands – admittedly, popular resort areas for pleasure boats, parties, and tourists. The *Wall Street Journal* published an article on the community's zeal in capitalizing on the monster tradition for Loch Ness-like prominence in the marketplace.

In 1989, the *Ottawa County Beacon*, climbed aboard the bandwagon with a contest to officially "name" the monster. "South Bay Bessie" came in first among 115 entries, although there are some who refer the tag "Lemmy," a phonetic spinoff of the acronym LEM, or Lake Erie Monster.

And, of course, there is always "*Obscura eriensis huronii.*" As mentioned prior, Ohio State's good-sport scientist Charles Herbendorf came up with the Latin designation, and he gamely indulged in this thought-experiment that biologists, naturalists, and limnologists have indulged ever since Nessie hit the headlines. Given known elements, such as water volume, quantity, and quality of fish – and assuming nothing will venture on land to feast on cattle or people – how many supposed "monsters" could a given lake host? Herbendorf added up the factors and concluded that, for whatever it's worth, Lake Erie has a capacity to support a colony of 175 "monsters" of 35 feet or so in length, and a couple of thousand kilograms in weight, give or take (2,000 kilograms equaling over 4,400 pounds).

In November 1990, the Huron Town Council passed a resolution designating themselves an official monster capture and control center. The Huron Lagoons marina owner had Lloyds of London underwrite a $102,700 reward for anyone able to catch South Bay Bessie (or any unknown aquatic animal at least 1,000 pounds and 30 feet long) alive. Nobody claimed the reward, likely offered in a promo spirit. A monster "holding pen" for any potential captive Lemmies or Bessies was really just a foot-deep pool to hold marina dredgings).

In 1994, local artist Tom Schofield and his family in Huron erected a fanciful, dragon-like sculpture of South Bay Bessie on the Huron River. They subsequently added a baby South Bay Bessie trailing the "parent," but this was stolen, and the earlier serpent, after years of turning heads of motorists on a nearby overpass, succumbed itself to the elements and, like the original inspiration, disappeared. Perhaps the most recent "evidence" of the Lake Erie

Monster is a mildly troubling rumor, that in August 2001, within one twenty-four-hour period, a man, a woman, and a child, all swimming in the same vicinity just outside Port Dover, were bitten by something beneath the water, something with toothy jaws six inches apart.

A doctor tentatively identified the culprit as the Bowfish or dogfish, which would seem a far likelier candidate, statistically, than a fossil whale, a dinosaur, or even a giant mutant freshwater sturgeon. Still, one wonders…

Mass sightings of more than one Lake Erie Monster at a time are rare – except at NHL hockey matches.

By the 21st century, the Lake Erie monster was quite famous indeed, even if the actual sightings had trailed off. A popular area restaurant was named after Lemmy; there are monster souvenirs, a gourmet beer. And the latest in a succession of Cleveland professional hockey-team franchises was christened the Lake Erie Monsters, with all the attendant commercial exploitation of the image of a reptilian cranium protruding from the surface of the world's twelfth biggest freshwater lake.

To the skeptical referees of science, the verdict on water monsters, in the Great Lakes or elsewhere, is disproven by lack of solid evidence. But the fans-cum-believers will continue to watch over the waters and continue to wonder about what abides, unseen in the deep.

Captain Nemo surveys his watery domain from the deck of the *Nautilus*, in an illustration from an early edition of *20,000 Leagues Under the Sea*, part of the collection of the Jules Verne House, a museum to the visionary author and his world in Tours, France.

"...In The Land of Submarines"

In Which a General Discussion of Submersible Watercraft on the Great Lakes Leads Us to the Remarkable Amphibious Exploits of a Certain Lodner Darvonitis Phillips. Family Excursions to the Bottom of Lake Michigan by a Cobbler's Son. A Mysterious Revelation in the Chicago River. Riddles Surrounding the Lost Legacies of L.D. Phillips Inspire the Not-Exactly-Rhetorical Question of Just How Many Submarines Can One Man Reasonably Misplace?

I have become fascinated with a set of news pictures taken for a Chicago newspaper in late 1915 – but, according to what I have gathered, never printed for the edification of readers at the time. The photographs are accessible now via a Chicago local-history archive on the World Wide Web.

I stare at the pictures, hypnotized, like those who come to gaze upon the *Mona Lisa* or a Van Gogh for hours. I would surmise they are on glass-plate negatives, probably five inches by seven inches, taken with a heavy camera, most likely set on a tripod or some other stable platform. Nonetheless, the lens was sharp, the photographer a skilled technician. The monochrome image is crisp and clear and can be magnified and explored to a degree that would be the envy of any digital shooter even now, nearly 100 years later.

The pictures show a work crew with a barge and a crane on the Chicago River hauling up from the water a...*thing*. A thing that looks so completely out of its proper time and place, it takes my breath away. I am reminded of Nigel Kneale's famous science-fiction teleplay *Quatermass and the Pit*, a thriller about a similar object unearthed in London during excavations for a subway line; in the fantasy script it turned out to be a long-buried alien rocketship, ancient and dangerous.

There is something rocket-like indeed about this anomaly in the Chicago River, or at least otherworldly. But it also bears a marked resemblance to another exotic type of ship, a submarine. And that is what it was taken to be – a submarine. In the Chicago River in the Edwardian Era, not the likeliest habitat for a submarine.

And if this is the submarine its proponents say it is, then it might have come to lay in that river long before these pictures were taken. Perhaps very long.

Submarines on the Great Lakes? Well, yes, of course there are submarines on the Great Lakes. In Cleveland a submarine called the USS *Cod* is a community and field-trip favorite, permanently moored near a lake-fronting small airport and the Rock and Roll Hall of Fame and Museum. One of the American fleet of WWII naval attack submarines built in Connecticut in 1942 as a response to the Japanese attack on Pearl Harbor, the diesel sub sank at least 12 enemy transports and battleships, sending 37,000 tons of the Empire of the Rising Sun to the bottom during eight patrols. The *Cod* undertook history's first submarine-to-submarine rescue, in July 1945, coming to the aid of a Dutch sub that had run aground on a reef, taking on the 56 Netherlanders and raising the population of the claustrophobic 312-foot *Cod* to a tight 153 men during the two-day trip to Subic Bay.

After serving as a postwar training vessel, she was saved from scrapping and/or target practice by a movement of Clevelanders who had grown fond of the *Cod* and opened to the public as a permanent memorial and museum in 1976. Her stature as the best-preserved and restored American Second World War sub on display was enhanced by the recent discovery of two *Cod* engines in nearby storage. Documentary crews have used her interior and conning tower as a backdrop for re-enactments.

At Chicago's Museum of Science and Industry a star attraction is the *U-505*, a diesel-powered German U-boat captured in battle during WWII, a deliberate strategy of a group of United States Navy men, including Lt. Col. Daniel Gallery, who had been engaged in anti-submarine operations in the north Atlantic and saw crippled but intact German submarines evacuated and scuttled by their crews. Deciding that nemesis sub could be recovered if boarders acted quickly enough, Gallery and his task force harassed and depth-charged the *U-505* off the coast of Africa. Once the German submariners escaped, an eight-man boarding party, working against the clock, entered the sub, closed the valves that were flooding her, and disarmed timed explosives meant to keep the boat and her technology and codes from Allied eyes. The sub was towed to Bermuda and studied under utmost secrecy.

Immediately after the war, the Navy planned to destroy the *U-505* in target practice. Daniel Gallery's brother informed the Chicago Museum of Science and Industry, who were hoping to obtain a surplus sub for public display. Via a public fundraising effort, the *U-505* was installed on the Chicago lakefront in 1954 as both a museum exhibit and memorial to casualties of the Atlantic fighting. Even her still-proud German manufacturers donated replacement parts to enable a fuller restoration. In 2004, after decades of outdoor display, the boat was relocated to a controlled underground environment, where she remains today – not merely the only submarine capture in warfare, but the only enemy vessel taken whole by the US Navy since Oliver Hazard Perry and the Battle of Lake Erie in 1813 (see Chapter 2).

Yes, there are submarines on the Great Lakes. But there have been submarines under the Great Lakes, for perhaps longer than most people know.

The heroic WWII submarine USS *Cod* in Cleveland, Ohio.

It happened in Chicago, decades earlier, a time when submarines on the order of the *Cod* or the *U-505* were still the stuff of Jules Verne science fiction. This "watershed" event in the secret history of Great Lakes submarines made banner headlines of the boisterous *Chicago Tribune* newspaper in the late autumn of 1915. It would create a number of regional myths and questions that still have not been answered to the satisfaction of historians.

A key figure in the incident was Chicago diver William "Frenchy" Deneau, of the Great Lakes Dredge and Dock Company, a man one would have to say had a most memorable year. In July of 1915, he was prominent in the melancholy operations that retrieved hundreds of drowned victims from the half-capsized pleasure ship *Eastland*, the worst nautical disaster in Great Lakes history (see Chapter 4). On November 23, Deneau was involved in a seemingly more prosaic exercise, laying underwater cable in the Chicago River near Rush Street Bridge.

The newspaper stories – which would subsequently shift and disagree with each other like so much unstable marl – initially claimed that, beneath three feet of mud, he had stubbed his toe on an object of considerable size. It was a tapered cigar- or spindle-shaped construction, about twelve meters in length. Deneau raised it intact from the water on December 20, with *Chicago Daily News* press photographers in attendance to record the weird sight. It looked like no familiar vessel or barge on the Great Lakes, or off.

Within a very short time the relic, dubbed the "Fool Killer," went on display on South State Street, with an admission charge of ten cents to see "the most intensely interesting exhibit ever shown in Chicago" and hear Deneau speak about it.

The strange object was, in time, said to be one of an indeterminate number of submarine ships and devices – some merely remaining schematics or patent applications, some actually built and used – by a little-known inventor named Lodner Darvonitis Phillips. He was born in New York state in 1825 to a family that had been cobblers and bootmakers for five generations. Depending on which of the scanty L.D. Phillips biographies one reads, he is described either as a genius ahead of his time or something of a dilettante idler and ill-fated dreamer. But there is general agreement that he deserves greater recognition as a pioneer and (somewhat hapless) champion of underwater exploration, travel, and warfare.

Though visions of peering and probing underwater in diving-bell-like assemblies date back to the ancient Greeks (and Alexander of Macedon beholding the sea from his own glass enclosure in 334 B.C.), the concepts of self-propelled, pressurized underwater vehicles do not begin until after the Renaissance. A Dutch inventor working for King James I tested three proto-submarines in the River Thames between 1620 and 1624. In 1634, two French priests, known to history as Father Mersenne and Father Fornier, created on paper the design for an underwater attack ship. But the American War for Independence saw the first actual application – or attempt – at using a self-powered submersible in naval battle.

In September, 1776, Ezra Lee piloted a hand-cranked, barrel-shaped vehicle aptly called the *Turtle*, invented by one David Bushnell of Connecticut. With dimensions of six feet by four feet, the *Turtle* was meant to churn along almost entirely submerged except for a small viewing-port (not advanced enough to be called a periscope) to attempt to drill into a hull and attach explosives unseen. The strategy of this unique secret weapon, the first mission of its kind in history, failed – although the *Turtle* would seem to have inspired a plot detail in the Hollywood classic *The Crimson Pirate*, as a Ben Franklin-style character during the great age of sail surfaces in a makeshift submarine to throw a bomb.

In the real world, more prototype submarines were to come. Steamboat inventor Robert Fulton created the *Nautilus*, tested in France in 1800 (with a sail for surface use) as a possible vehicle for Napoleon Bonapart's navy in laying ocean mines, but it was never deployed. The Russian Karl Shilder's 1834 submarine could be armed with rockets. An 1851 German submarine can be seen today in a Dresden museum. During the Civil War the Confederacy sent one submarine into battle, the *Hunley*. In February, 1864, the hand-cranked ship used its one explosive charge to annihilate the *Housatonic*, a Union warship blockading Charleston. Then, after signaling to shore via lamplight of the success of her offensive, the *Hunley* sank, for reasons yet unknown, taking her entire crew with her. The short-lived naval forces of Jefferson Davis earned immortality for the first successful, if tragic, attack using a submersible vessel.

In the middle of the 1800s, the standard technology of underwater exploration was still the basic diving bell.

The Union, meanwhile, also entertained military submarine plans. A little-known submarine called the *Alligator* was prepared and tested and possibly even inspected by President Abraham Lincoln. But, while being towed by a Union schooner, the *Alligator* was cut loose during a storm and lost off the Atlantic coast. Fortunately, nobody was on board. It is fascinating historical trivia that the French immigrant who designed the *Alligator*, an engineer called Brutus Villeroi, taught mathematics at the school in France attended by the young Jules Verne – though the degree of interaction between the two visionaries remains unknown. What we do know, of course, is that Jules Verne's novel, *20,000 Leagues Under the Sea*, published in 1870, held readers worldwide spellbound with its renegade hero Captain Nemo and the potential of the submarine.

Embedded like algae between these seafaring milestones, however, are the few confirmed facts and much speculation and myth about L.D. Phillips, the Nemo of the Great Lakes. He moved west with his family from New York, the dynasty ultimately established a bustling shoe factory in Michigan City, Indiana, then delved into farming. Lodner seemed not to have had much interest in either pursuit, instead taking up inventions. It may or may not be significant that L.D. Phillips had a talent of being able to sign his name backwards as neatly as frontwards. A similar capability is recorded of Leonardo Da Vinci, who could do mirror-writing free-handed.

Early experiments of Lodner Darvonitis Phillips come from scant, but much-quoted, anecdotes provided by the Phillips descendants, prompted by a mid-20th-century boast. In June of the fateful year of 1941, with a World War looming on the horizon that would partially be fought underwater by the likes of the USS *Cod* and the *U-505*, the Bay Shipbuilding Company proudly announced its completion and launching of the first submarine on the Great Lakes. Not so fast, responded some old maritime hands. Gustave Phillips, Lodner's grand-nephew, told the Michigan City *Argus* newspaper that Lodner actually tested out a submarine on Lake Michigan *nearly a full century before*.

Phillips attempted to launch a submarine of his own design at Trail Creek in Michigan City in 1845. It was mostly wooden, covered with copper sheeting, and it held a hand-operated pressure cylinder which controlled the buoyancy. Sitting inside the vessel, Phillips moved the craft along with an oar-like pole that passed through a (theoretically) water-tight, flexible rubber gasket. Thus the thing could be "punted" along the bottom. It seems that the unnamed ship survived a few tests, but finally either sank or collapsed and flooded. Phillips, according to one account, had reached a depth of twenty feet down, and he managed to swim free of the wreck.

Not long afterwards, Lodner married Maria Holland, from Dublin, Ireland, and the couple had the first of three children. Phillips' submarine experiments continued, however, with his father and brothers primarily underwriting his operating expenses.

In 1851, in a story much-quoted and given credence by the United States Navy, Phillips brought forth a submarine later judged to be the most successful submersible, self-driven craft yet developed. The boat, according to one source, was sixty feet long, seven feet across, and bore some kind of on-board air-supply to allow immersion for about four hours, even assuming up to twenty or thirty people on board. Two glass observation domes admitted light, and there was a provision for an artificial cabin light for deep descent – as well as reflectors that could cast illumination outside the vessel. For propulsion, either human muscle would turn the crank that operated the propeller and gave the craft its top speed of four-and-a-half knots, or a method of "electro-magnetism" invented by Phillips would do the work.

As an unusual safety feature the submarine bore a "thimble," a sort of secondary hull or nose-cone loosely worn over the bow. In the event of a collision or the bow somehow getting stuck or ensnarled, the ship had merely to reverse the propeller; the sub would back out, leaving the "thimble" behind.

One storied day that summer, Phillips is said to have taken Maria and their two children on board the vessel and explored the bottom of Lake Michigan. But L.D. Phillips was cognizant that such a ship had more uses than just providing a most unique family outing. He also developed a "six-pounder" artillery gun designed to load and shoot underwater. In tests on Lake Michigan, a number of boats were anchored down, and Phillips took a gun-mounted submarine down to practice-fire his shells through the wooden hulls. He would later proclaim successful sinkings or full-scale destruction of the targets.

In addition, the L.D. Phillips submarine now boasted a special hinged bow design that allowed the possibility of handling objects or cutting timbers outside of the vessel and deploying tools for performing salvage and recovery operations. Phillips announced a successful test in which an operator aboard the submarine cut through a piece of timber fourteen inches square.

In 1853, Phillips took either this submarine, or another one of similar design (possibly powered by a steam engine) to Lake Erie, for further tests. On this occasion, he sought to reach a shipwreck 155 feet down. The facts are slightly contradictory – one Phillips relative thought the mission went to Lake Huron – but the majority of the accounts claim that Phillips' target was the *Atlantic*, a steamship that, in the summer of 1852, was carrying about 600 immigrant passengers west when she was rammed in the predawn hours by the freighter *Ogdensburgh* (see Chapter 4). The *Atlantic* went to the bottom five to six miles south of the Canadian shore of Port Ontario. As with many similar sinkings of immigrant-laden ships, rumors persisted of personal treasure and fortunes going down with the victims. The potential reward here was rumored to total as much as $36,000 – nearly a million dollars by modern standards.

For Phillips and his new craft to recover any of that would be quite a coup for the infant submarine field – and a balm for Phillips' chronic debts.

For the expedition, Phillips worked in partnership with Elliott Harrington of New York. A few years previously they had used Phillips' dive armor to seek the body of a farmer who had drowned in Lake Erie. That particular expedition ended in failure, as would the attempt to use a submarine to pry salvage from the *Atlantic*. At 100 feet down, Phillips' submarine developed severe leaks, and Lodner was forced to surface and evacuate. Apparently, Phillips miscalculated the weight of his craft when it was flooded, and the ropes towing the sub broke. Thus was the singular boat lost to Erie's cold embrace. A few years later, in 1856, Harrington, in diving armor, recovered a safe from the *Atlantic* containing more than $30,000, though rival court claims ate away at most of his profits.

Even before the *Atlantic* setback, however, Phillips had felt comfortable enough with his submarine test runs and technology to apply for an official US Patent. Patent Number 9389, for "Steering Submarine Vessels," with schematics, was granted November 9, 1852. According to a letter Phillips sent to United States Navy in April of that year, he had built two propeller-driven submarines and had been operating them in front of reliable witnesses since 1847 – a confusion in dates, as Phillips was known to be attempting sub launchings in 1845. Biographer Patricia Gruse Harris proposes that Phillips did not wish to mention the early, pole-pushed invention that came to such an ignoble end.

Phillips informed the Navy Department that he could manufacture a submarine for the armed forces costing $800 – while the closest thing he had to a competitor, "a Frenchman" (this almost certainly must have been Brutus Villeroi) in New York, consumed $9,000 in the construction of his own submarine.

In a dismissive reply, a Navy bureaucrat named Graham relayed a response that "the boats used by the Navy go *on* and not *under* the water."

It must have been a sharp disappointment. The marine experiments had strained the family finances badly. Phillips relocated to Chicago – ahead of a sheriff who tried to serve him papers at his former Michigan City address. His wife and children came with him to Chicago, but after Maria died there in 1862, we are told, he spent less time on family matters and more on inventions.

In the heart of the great city, L.D. Phillips could be seen testing his ideas in the Chicago River, with throngs of observers as his audience. In addition to the submarine, Lodner now fabricated an armored suit, to allow a man to walk beneath the water's surface, principally for salvage operations. In a typical display, later described by Lodner's son, the inventor would put on his gear on board a boat and have an assistant hurl the anchor overboard. Phillips would then enter the water, breathing via a tube, walk to the anchor, attach inflatable canvas bags, and float the heavy object to the surface. On October 14, 1856, the US Patent Office granted Phillips his "Diving Armor" patent.

Phillips undertook a diversity of inventions, including a diving bell for underwater salvage; a wool-carding device; a machine to do the work of a plasterer; and a mechanism or two for buttons and other schemes of fabric-fastening. But none made his fortune, and, according to Harris, there is reason to suspect that the wool-carding idea was stolen from Phillips and enriched the pockets of a large company.

There has always been confusion over just how many fantastic machines Lodner Darvonitis Phillips did physically produce. Author Adam Selzer guesses that at least four submarines made it past the blueprint stage, the first sinking at Trail Creek, another in Lake Erie, and another lost in the Chicago River...maybe.

In Lodner's imagination, however, the size of the Phillips submarine fleet knew no bounds. Now living in New York City as the Civil War blazed, he continued his correspondence with the Navy. In 1864, he proposed to Secretary of the Navy Gideon Wells a quartet of submarine warships. One was a forty-footer whose five-man crew had the option to remain underwater and breathing for twenty-four hours if necessary. The vessel would be able to approach enemy ships by stealth and physically attach a bomb (a mission the *Hunley* succeeded in executing) or unleash a sort of underwater mine. Another was a 120-foot long model, a steam-powered sub with 3-inch armor plating and a 20-man crew able to remain submerged for 5 full days. Another was the archetypal "infernal machine," festooned with an amphibious arsenal of guns able to shoot underwater or above the surface, and capable of sending rockets arcing to 3 miles' distance. These ships would all do well for near-shore, river, lake, and harbor incursions, but for open sea he envisioned a true leviathan, 200 feet long and bearing heavy artillery.

The 1952 Hollywood costume drama *Mutiny* fancifully depicted an archaic, hand-cranked wooden submarine with attributes of both the Confederate *Hunley* and the "Marine Cigar," as a secret American weapon of the War of 1812.

Biographer Patricia Gruse Harris noted that the reaction of the Permanent Commission of the Navy Department was guarded. Despite the *Hunley*, despite Phillips' own weapons tests on the Great Lakes, they declared they knew of no practical demonstration of submarine warfare. Nonetheless, documents indicate an appropriation was set aside to finance US Navy construction of one of the more modest submarines in Phillips' arsenal. And then...nothing seems to have happened. Or, at least, there are no records yet discovered, and the Civil War ended without an obvious L.D. Phillips contribution to the Union cause.

One story, circulated by Lodner Phillips' granddaughter in 1912, but unverified anywhere else, claims that the British government made an offer of $50,000 for a Phillips submarine that had been successfully demonstrated to Her Majesty's naval officers. Phillips refused to sell, on principle, to a foreign power – whereupon the British scuttled the vessel. The tale seems unlikely on numerous counts – perhaps the smallest objection being that submarines in general found disfavor with the upper classes of the Royal Navy and especially Queen Victoria herself. The notion of a warship moving stealthy, invisible against an opponent, was considered sneaky, non-chivalrous...un-British. In any case, the best evidence that Patricia Gruse Harris could uncover suggested that a Phillips collaborator took submarine plans to England to show, but could find no support.

Nonetheless, the granddaughter's account continued; after this, Phillips built another submarine, for a benefactor named Frederick Peck. Unfortunately, Peck had enemies, far more personal ones than vulnerable wooden-hulled warships. In the late 1860s, two ex-convicts, blaming Peck for their prison terms, invaded Peck's offices in New York City when Phillips was there. In the fight that resulted, both marauders were thrown down a flight of stairs, one to his death. But the exertion caused a recurrence of chronic "consumption" (usually the euphemism for tuberculosis) that had been plaguing Phillips for some months.

He died on October 15, 1869, at age 43, with a medical verdict of "phthisis pulmonalis," although one can only surmise what his respiratory system might have been like from years of experimenting with underwater-breathing apparatuses and do-it-yourself air-purification rigs for his submarines. In death as well, a myth attached itself to the exploits of Lodner D. Phillips – that he had drowned in Lake Erie along with one of his fantastic underwater crafts.

He may as well have been, in a sense, for his gravesite in Green-Wood Cemetery in Brooklyn, far from the family left behind Michigan City, Indiana, goes unmarked. Not long afterward the devouring flames of the Great Chicago Fire of October 8, 1871, would eradicate many vital municipal records covering the period when Phillips lived, worked, and researched in that city – documents which could have clarified many questions to come later.

Down the years, his adult children would remember relics of the Phillips submarines – miniature models, hemispherical "reflectors" for casting light into the depths – used around the homestead as toys or bowls, or simply souvenirs. Eventually, all such relics were lost.

Except for some saved documents and patent plans (and even those often incomplete), the most enduring evidence that Lodner Darvonitis Phillips, a son of shoemakers, excelled – perhaps beyond anyone else in his era at designing and building submarines – remains mere word-of-mouth and reputation.

Unless...the extraordinary object hauled up out of the Chicago River in late 1915 was indeed Lodner Phillips' lost underwater man-o-war "Fool Killer." And therein lies another twisted tale that raises as many questions as answers.

One of the few photographs of a Lodner D. Phillips "Marine Cigar" – if that is indeed the identity of this enigmatic object at all. The raising of the "Foolkiller" from tragedy-stained waters of the Chicago River in late 1915. *Courtesy of the Chicago Historical Society.*

For one thing, Phillips had never been known to dub any of his submersibles "Fool Killer"; instead, he called his masterpiece submarine of 1851 the "Marine Cigar." The designation "Foolkiller" – an archaic general slang, referring to a sort of boogey-man-ish figure who preyed on those stupid and reckless enough to deserve death – was applied to a series of odd vessels developed by Peter Nissen, a Chicago accountant, eccentric and self-styled daredevil once mentioned with some frequency in the city's press.

Nissen built a series of "Foolkillers" – the first two being torpedo-like cork boats custom-designed for the purpose of shooting the treacherous rapids of the Niagara River. *Foolkiller No. 3* was a bizarre canvas inflatable, holding a sort of hammock in which Nissen resided as the machine more or less rolled across the surface of a lake. In December 1904, Nissen set off from Chicago determined to cross Lake Michigan in the *Foolkiller No. 3*. He was found dead from exposure, not far from the collapsed shroud of his invention, at Stevensville, Michigan.

When Deneau pulled the cigar-shaped wooden object from the Chicago River, the *Chicago Tribune*'s initial report claimed that the eccentric Nissen had owned this unique vehicle as well. In a chronology, sketchy at best, he had not in fact built the submersible "Foolkiller," but rather purchased it in the late 1800s, after the original inventor, only identified as a man from New York...drowned while testing it on the Great Lakes.

A month later, however, the *Tribune* printed the revelation that bones had been found aboard the "Foolkiller submarine." While cleaning the mud-choked interior, Deneau and his collaborators had discovered the remains: some human, some canine. The newspaper now wrote that the machine's out-of-town inventor tested it in the Chicago River in the 1870s, but it sank. Two decades later, a William Nissen – the earlier mis-attribution to Peter Nissen never clarified in those fast-and-loose days of journalism – raised the craft, restored, and relaunched it. But then, at some point in the 1890s, Nissen and his wooden submarine simply disappeared. A local authority also spoke ambiguously of an experimental submarine of some sort being lost in the Chicago River fifteen years prior. At least until being rediscovered by "Frenchy" Deneau in the aftermath of the *Eastland* capsizing (and at least one official ruled out the "Foolkiller" as having been the rumored, uncharted "obstruction" in the Chicago River that inspired the *Eastland*'s mishap and caused the Great Lakes' deadliest disaster).

Deneau, it seems, was quite a colorful waterfront character in the Chicago press. After 1915, he took to calling himself "Captain" Deneau. Articles about him gave three separate locations along the river pinpointing where he "found" the "Foolkiller" submarine; either the reporters got it wrong or Deneau could not, for some reason, keep his story straight. He was also in debt for alimony. Even into the 1950s "Captain" Deneau occasionally bobbed up in the Chicago newspapers, making bigger than life boasts and inaccurate statements about the *Eastland*.

Cecil Adams, latter-day author of the popular syndicated column "The Straight Dope," invested what he himself said was an inordinate amount of time in trying to disentangle the L.D. Phillips/Foolkiller enigma. Adams has concluded that discovery of the relic submarine was a staged, for-profit hoax –

with at least some of the Chicago press, prominently the *Tribune* merrily going along for the ride. The photographer for a rival paper, the *Chicago Daily News*, took extraordinary pictures of the raising of the "submarine" but the *Daily News* printed neither the images nor one word about it; Adams surmises they just didn't believe any of it. As with the much later "flying saucer crash" at Roswell, New Mexico, the conflicting story of the ship's origins and the possible bodies aboard changed over time – as if in calculation to fuel further publicity and ticket sales to the exhibition. And the fact that a marine archaeological discovery so important could be shunted off straightaway to a sideshow-exhibition tour fairly reeks of premeditated fraud.

But how could Deneau have pulled it off? Adams theorizes that as a seasoned salvager and diver (if not a real "captain"), the rascally Deneau had knowledge of other amateur submersibles built in and around the Chicago area, available to pass off as his own incredible find connected with the conveniently dead Peter Nissen. A George Baker of Chicago had tested one wooden sub in Lake Michigan near Calumet in 1893; Richard Raddatz of Oshkosh, Wisconsin, tried a sixty-five-foot cylindrical submarine off Milwaukee in 1900; and there were a few others.

Or did Deneau indeed manage to put his hands on a lost submarine of Lodner Phillips – perhaps the one that had been built for Frederick Peck? Or the British government? Or the Union during the Civil War, or some other client? Which would mean, more or less, that a genuine specimen of the world's oldest operating submarine had been passed off as a fake one. Even Cecil Adams admits that of all the known candidates, the 1852 US Patent drawings of the self-propelled Phillips "Marine Cigar" most closely mirror the tapered thing in the *Chicago Daily News* photo archives, whereas other known submarines of the era (including Lodner's earlier designs) were more or less football- or barrel-shaped, or nowhere near the requisite size.

By rights, the 1915 relic raised from the Chicago River's bed would be a Holy Grail of marine historians, much like the *Hunley* became when the Confederate hero ship was finally located in the Atlantic off Charleston and, in the 1990s, raised to the surface (the skeletons of the crew inside). But nobody knows what became of Captain Deneau's roadside attraction.

Its latter voyages can be traced only to 1916. Sold or leased by Deneau, the "Foolkiller" made an appearance barnstorming around the Midwest with something called Parker's Greatest Shows, a traveling carnival and Skeeball emporium operated by one Charles W. Parker. The show visited Oelwein, Iowa, with a menagerie of marvels, including a freak show. The river relic was listed on the bill as "The Submarine or Fool Killer," and purported to be the first submarine ever built.

But the carnival circuit was one in which a profitable attraction, if unavailable, could simply be copied or fabricated for the gawkers and the rubes. P.T. Barnum notoriously had several stone effigies traveling in different territories, each tubthumped as the actual "Cardiff Giant"; in truth Barnum never even had access to the original "Cardiff Giant" (which, as every follower of hoaxes knows, was itself a fake) and just mass-produced his own.

Another Chicago newspaper, the *Examiner*, stated that the "Fool Killer" submarine was back on display in that city's Riverview Park a month afterwards. From that point on, the trail of the Foolkiller (or a Foolkiller) fades. It may well have been broken up for scrap or abandoned somewhere, forgotten.

For the adventurers seeking a preserved L.D. Phillips submarine, there is still a possible option. The stories about this Nemo of the Great Lakes claim that he used one of his creations to attempt to recover booty from the *Atlantic* in Lake Erie, but lost the submarine in the vicinity. The location of the *Atlantic* is well known to wreck divers, including Mike Fletcher, a longtime construction-diver and salvager, who rediscovered the sunken steamer in 1983.

There, Fletcher beheld on the partially caved-in deck of the *Atlantic* a peculiar, "tank"-shaped object. No, he said, it was not a submarine, but rather a late 19th-century flotation apparatus, left behind by an earlier, abortive attempt to raise the *Atlantic*. This additional relic, said Fletcher, was mistaken for the L.D. Phillips sub by a rival team of salvors – in fact, lawsuits in the 1980s and 1990s over salvage rights to the *Atlantic* were so excruciating that Fletcher left the field entirely for the more sedate occupation of underwater documentary filmmaking. But the case left rumors that, indeed, the lost "Marine Cigar" had been sighted.

In fact, said Fletcher, he himself espied nothing in the immediate vicinity of the *Atlantic* that resembled the ill-fated Phillips submarine in 1983. Fletcher made repeat sorties to the *Atlantic* over the years and was especially chagrined that in a relatively short amount of time, that particular area of Lake Erie had become heavily silted over, the *Atlantic* all but buried. If a nearby "Marine Cigar" had been difficult to discern before, it would be impossible to see now.

And did one sink there at all? There is a frustrating gap in the historical record; the *Cleveland Gazette* newspaper of 1853 carried a report of the "Marine Cigar" arriving by railway to embark on the intrepid quest – but no follow-up story. Some blanks were filled in – partially – by an obscure article interviewing William Phillips, a retired lighthouse keeper and son of Lodner D. Phillips. Among the old light-keeper's reminiscences was adventuring with his father in a homemade, hand-cranked submarine, built primarily of oak, to explore an unnamed shipwreck in the deepest part of Lake Erie (the *Atlantic* lies in the deepest part of the generally shallow Erie). At the 100-foot depth, the Phillips submarine began leaking, and father and son had a narrow escape from the flooded vessel. Then the rope towing the submersible broke.

Mike Fletcher postulates that L.D. Phillips, seeking backers for his submarine technology, found this outcome so appalling and humiliating he simply kept it out of the newspapers and any official record, just as he minimized his short-lived, pole-pushed 1845 submarine. Only by scraps and innuendo can we conclude with certainty that a "Marine Cigar," in one piece and likely in a good state of preservation thanks to the freshwater environment, lies somewhere near the *Atlantic* in Lake Erie. But the challenge, explains Fletcher, who has tackled many lost underwater relics with cutting-edge instruments, is that the "Marine Cigar" was mostly wooden, with minimal metal fittings and gears. Its metallic "signature" would be overwhelmed by the mass of metal represented by the nearby sunken *Atlantic* (not to mention the interloping old salvage tank).

...And, there is always the remote possibility – accepting, of course, Sherlock Holmes' famous line that by ruling out the impossible, whatever remains, however improbable, must be the answer – that by means unknown, the lost "Marine Cigar" in Lake Erie somehow found its way into the Chicago River. Perhaps to be rigged in 1915 as a "discovery" by Frenchy Deneau and his unscrupulous syndicate and taken on the carnival circuit.

The Phillips family maintains that Lodner did indeed lose a submarine in the Chicago River as well, but details are lacking. Could there be any conceivable connection to the agreement, half-hearted though it may have been, by the United State Navy to construct a submarine of L.D. Phillips' design? Officially, the first US Navy sub was the *Holland*, launched in 1900 and named for her designer, John P. Holland, of New Jersey. Officially, that is...

The Five Sisters keep to themselves many secrets, and this is only one of the most tantalizing, that someday, somehow, an incredible artifact may come to light from the depths, to rightfully join the *Cod* and the *U-505*, and demonstrating Lodner D. Phillips' contribution to a world in which boats of the world's navies do indeed go *under* as well as *on* the water.

Ojibwe author, educator, activist and artist Lois Beardslee preserves traditional native arts and thought in diverse media, including storytelling. Her work has been widely exhibited, from the Royal Ontario Museum to the Smithsonian Institution. This mixed-media panel, entitled Nibing, incorporates birch bark in a representation of summer on the Great Lakes. *Courtesy of Lois Beardslee.*

Afterword

I.
The Underwater Panther and the Thunderbirds of Lake Superior

By Lois Beardslee

We Ojibwe people are rooted in a culture based upon pragmatism, survival in a cold and wet climate with bountiful resources to be harvested and the need for mnemonic devices for teaching success and safety through methods proven by generations of trial and error. Our word, *manido*, often translated as "spirit," actually means "mystery." It is used to explain phenomena we cannot explain. Names, characters, and ancestors are tied to these phenomena as well as to things we understand and want to teach. Among the most misunderstood characters and mnemonic devices of our culture are Mishi Bizhou, the underwater panther, and the Aniimkiyag, the thunderbirds. By tradition, when one represents one of these characters, one must represent the other, as they are constantly in opposition to one another, and one character is usually in opposition to the other. Our mnemonic device for their opposition is to anthropomorphize these animals by saying that they are jealous of one another and must be given equal attention. The characters each represent forces of wind and water on the lakes, and they constantly work against one another. Ignoring one of these potential forces on the water could be life-threatening on a body of water as large as Lake Superior, so it has always been essential for our storytellers, parents, and teachers to make sure that the two characters are tied together in the minds of our children and stay that way into adulthood.

Mishi Bizhou, the largest of the wild cats of the Great Lakes, has a long, thick tail that it uses for balance, just like a house cat. Sometimes when this mountain lion, or cougar, stands still watching other animals, only its tail twitches. The tail can be moved in great wave-like motions, just like old swells on the Great Lakes. So Mishi Bizhou represents energy stored up in old waves and large swells from previous hours or even days. Such waves are often left over from old storms, even though the wind has changed direction to offshore and the air seems calm.

We have a saying on Lake Superior, "When you take your coat off, the wind is about to change direction." There is a dead calm in the moments when the wind shifts. People in watercraft find themselves suddenly warm and shedding clothing, often lulled by the softening action of old swells. But things never stay calm for long out on the lake. A sharp wind can seem to come out of nowhere. If a sharp chop appears on the surface moving in the opposite direction of the old swells, we say that the thunderbirds are beating their wings. The new wind has a short, repetitive nature that moves a canoe or a boat differently than old swells. If the wind becomes strong, navigating between multiple different wave heights, widths, and directions can be an art form.

People can find themselves riding into short chop while rolling sideways in an old swell that is pushing in a different direction from the wind on the surface. There is a tension between the water and the wind. This can overturn a watercraft or push it onto rocks or far out into open water away from shore. Sometimes small boats have to ride between opposing forces of water, wind, and stored energy by snaking and backtracking like a surfer following crests and dips, but with the addition of short waves pounding at the bow. When that happens, we say that we are riding with the Michigaamigag. These are underwater snakes with antlers. They move smoothly and quickly, but running into their antlers can be as deadly as hitting a rock reef that has been exposed by a deep wave swell or striking a floating log. The Michigaamigag live along the shores of lakes and rivers. Sometimes you can see them when the light is low at dawn or dusk. They look a lot like old logs with branches sticking up out of them. But they're not. They are alive.

II.
"Lost on the *Lady Elgin*"
Lyrics by Henry Work

Up from the poor man's cottage,
Forth from the mansion door,
Sweeping across the waters and echoing 'long the shore,
Caught by the morning breezes,
Borne on the evening gale;
Cometh a voice of mourning, a sad and solemn wail.

Refrain:
Lost on the Lady Elgin!
Sleeping to wake no more!
Number'd in that three hundred,
Who failed to reach the shore.

Oh! 'Tis the cry of children
Weeping for parents gone;
Children who slept at evening
But orphans awoke at dawn.
Sisters for brother weeping,
Husbands for missing wives
– Such are the ties dissever'd
With those three hundred lives.

Staunch was the noble steamer,
Precious the freight she bore;
Gaily she loosed her cables,
A few short hours before.
Grandly she swept our harbor,
Joyfully rang her bell;
Little thought we e'er morning
'Twould toll so sad a knell.

III.
"Who is John Maynard?"
Lyrics by Theodore Fontane

"John Maynard was our helmsman true.
To solid land he carried us through.
He saved our lives, our noble king.
He died for us; his praise we sing.
John Maynard."
From Detroit to Buffalo
As mist sprays her bow like flakes of snow
Over Lake Erie the *Swallow* takes flight
And every heart is joyful and light.
In the dusk, the passengers all
Can already make out the dim landfall,
And approaching John Maynard, their hearts free of care,
They ask of their helmsman, "Are we almost there?"
He looks around and toward the shore:
"Still thirty minutes...a half hour more."
All hearts are happy, all hearts are light—
Then out of the hold comes a cry of fright.
"Fire!" it is, that terrified shout.

From the cabin and hatch black smoke pours out.
Smoke, then fire and flames aglow,
And still twenty minutes to Buffalo.
And the passengers, in a colorful crowd
Stand pressed together on the bow.
Up on the bow there is still air and light
But the smoke at the helm forms a thick, dark night.
"Where are we? Where?" the men must know,
And still fifteen minutes to Buffalo.
The wind grows strong but the smoke cloud stays.
To the helm the captain turns his gaze.
The helmsman is hidden by the raging fires
But through the bullhorn the captain enquires:
"Still there, John Maynard?"
"Yes, sir. I am."
"Onto the beach! Into the surf!"
"Yes, sir. That's my plan."
And the people cry: "Hold on! Hallo!"
And still ten minutes to Buffalo.
"Still there, John Maynard?" And the answer is clear,
Though with dying voice: "Yes, sir. I'm still here."
And in the surf, rocks, obstacles afloat,
Into their midst he plunges the boat.
To be saved, it's the only way to go.
Salvation: the shores of Buffalo!
The fire is out. The ship's run aground.
All are saved. Only one can't be found.
The bells ring out, their notes all fly
From churches and chapels to heaven on high.
The city is still but for funeral bells.
For one service only the sad sound swells:
In the procession ten thousand go by,
Or maybe more – and not one dry eye.
With layers of flowers the grave they soften.
Under more flowers they bury the coffin.
With golden script in marble stone
The city has its tribute shown:
"Here lies John Maynard! In smoke and fire
He held fast to the wheel; he did not tire.
He saved our lives, our noble king.
He died for us; his praise we sing.
John Maynard!"

Translated by Julie and Amy Huberman © 1996. Used by permission.

IV.
"Minnie Quay"

A traditional Lake Huron ballad with many variations in the lyrics. Some versions instead call the heroine "Winnie Gray." It seems only recent rewrites make reference to Minnie returning as a ghost.

'Twas in the town of Forester,
Along the sandy shore,
The voice of one poor Minnie Quay
We'll never hear no more.

Her soul is sweetly resting
For the Judgment Day to come,
When all shall render up accounts,
And the Judge pronounce our doom.

This fair maid was only sixteen,
She was scarcely in her bloom,
When her parents they got angry
And wished her in her tomb.

They said they wished that she was dead,
For some young man one day
Went and told an untruthful story
About poor Minnie Quay.

One day her parents went away
And left her all alone,
Alone with her little brother,
Until they should return.

Little did they think when they'd return
They'd find their daughter dead,
Gone to a land that is far fairer,
Where no more tears are shed.

'Twas on the twenty-sixth of April
Her parents went away.
Down by the side of Lake Huron
This fair one she did stray,

A-pondering on the dreadful scene
Which quickly must pass by,
For she had now determined
In a watery grave to lie.

She waved her hand to Forester
As if to say good-by;
Then quickly in Lake Huron
Her body it did lie.

Before anyone could render help,
Could lend a helping hand,
Her spirit it was borne away
Unto the Promised Land.

Now sweetly she is resting
In a cold and silent grave.
If her parents had not condemned her,
This fair one might have been saved.

But again her friends will meet her
If by the Savior they are led
To a land that is far better,
Where no farewell tears are shed.

Bibliography

Altoff, Gerald T. *Oliver Hazard Perry and the Battle of Lake Erie*. Put-In Bay, Ohio: The Perry Group, 1999.

Barrows, Edward M. *The Great Commodore*. Freeport, New York: Books For Libraries Press, 1935.

Barry, James P. *Ships of the Great Lakes*. Holt, Michigan: Thunder Bay Press, 2nd Edition 1996.

Bien, Laura. "Ypsi's Submarine Diver: The wreck of the steamship *Atlantic*." *Ann Arbor Chronicle*, May 13, 2010.

Bielski, Ursula. *Chicago Haunts: Ghostlore of the Windy City*. Chicago, Illinois: Lake Claremont Press, 1998.

Bishop, Hugh. *Haunted Lake Superior*. Duluth, Minnesota: Lake Superior Port Cities, 2003.

Bishop, Hugh. *Haunted Minnesota*. Duluth, Minnesota: Lake Superior Port Cities, 2006.

Bonansinga, Jay. *The Sinking of the* Eastland*: America's Forgotten Tragedy*. New York, New York: Citadel, 2004.

Bourrie, Mark. *Many a Midnight Ship*. Ann Arbor, Michigan: University of Michigan Press, 2005.

Bowen, Dana Thomas. *Memories of the Lakes*. Cleveland, Ohio: Lakeside Printing Company, 1946.

Bowen, Dana Thomas. *Shipwrecks of the Lakes*. Cleveland, Ohio: Lakeside Printing Company, 1952.

Boyer, Dwight. *Ghost Ships of the Great Lakes*. New York, New York: Dodd Mead & Company, 1968.

Boyer, Dwight. *True Tales of the Great Lakes*. New York, New York: Dodd Mead & Company, 1971.

Boyer, Dwight. *Strange Adventures of the Great Lakes*. New York, New York: Dodd Mead & Company, 1974.

Boyer, Dwight. *Ships and Men of the Great Lakes*. New York, New York: Dodd Mead & Company, 1977.

Bruseth, James E., and Toni S. Turner. *From a Watery Grave: The Discovery and Excavation of La Salle's Shipwreck* La Belle. College Station, Texas: Texas A&M University Press Consortium, 2005.

Cassady, Charles. *Cleveland Ghosts*. Atglen, Pennsylvania: Schiffer, 2008.

Cassady, Charles. *Paranormal Great Lakes*. Atglen, Pennsylvania: Schiffer, 2009.

Charney, Theodore S. "The *Rouse Simmons* and the Port of Chicago." *Inland Seas*, Winter, 1987.

Clements, Todd. *Haunts of Mackinac*. Grosse Pointe, Michigan: House of Hawthorne Publishing, 2006.

Coles, Harry L. *The War of 1812*. Chicago, Illinois: University of Chicago Press, 1965.

Columbo, John Robert. *Mysterious Canada*. Garden City, New York: Doubleday, 1988.

Columbo, John Robert. *True Canadian Ghost Stories*. Toronto, Ontario: Prospero Books, 2003.

Dukes. Howard. "Book brings Indiana Dunes legend to life." *South Bend Tribune*, September 11, 2011.

Edwards, Janet Zenke. *Diana of the Dunes*. Charleston, South Carolina: The History Press, 2010.

Ellis, William Donohue. *Land of the Inland Seas*. Palo Alto, California: American West Publishing Company, 1974.

Ewinger, James. "Cleveland's Ullman Sails repairs historic brig *Niagara*'s sails." *The Plain Dealer*, June 8, 2012.

Flesher, John. "Divers begin Lake Michigan excavation in search of lost 17th century ship, the *Griffin*." *Associated Press Wire Service*, June 15, 2013.

Forrester, C.S. *The Age of Fighting Sail*. Garden City, New York: Doubleday, 1956.

Godfrey, Linda S. *Weird Michigan*. New York, New York: Sterling Publishers, 2006.

Gutsche, Andrea, and Cindy Bisaillon. *Mysterious Islands: Forgotten Tales of the Great Lakes*. Toronto, Canada: Lynx Images, 1999.

Harris, Patricia Gruse. *Great Lakes' First Submarine: L.D. Phillips' "Fool Killer"* (2nd Edition). Michigan City, Indiana: Michigan City Historical Society, 2010.

Hauck, Dennis William. *Haunted Places: The National Directory*. New York, New York: Penguin Books, 2002.

Havighurst, Walter. *The Great Lakes Reader*. New York, New York: MacMillan, 1966.

Hertal, Captain Robert. *The* Edmund Fitzgerald – *Lost With All Hands*. Spring Lake, Michigan: River Road Publications, 1999.

Hopkins, L.E. *1850: Death on Erie*. Baltimore, Maryland: PublishAmerica, 2011.

Hoyt, Edwin P. *The Tragic Commodore: The Story of Oliver Hazard Perry*. New York, New York: Abelard-Schuman, 1966.

Jackson, Robert. *Submarines of the World*. New York, New York: Barnes & Noble, 2000.

Jacobson, Bonnie, editor. *Cleveland in Prose and Poetry*. Cleveland, Ohio: League Books, 2005.

Kantar, Andrew. *29 Missing*. East Lansing, Michigan: Michigan University Press, 1998.

Kaczmarek, Dale. *Windy City Ghosts*. Alton, Illinois: Whitechapel Productions Press, 2000.

Keefe, Bill. *The Five Sisters*. Algonac, Michigan: Reference Publications, 1991.

Kohl, Chris. *Treacherous Waters: Kingston's Shipwrecks*. Chicago, Illinois: Seawolf Publications, 1997.

Kohl, Chris. *Shipwreck Tales of the Great Lakes*. Chicago, Illinois: Seawolf Publications, 2004.

Lankford, Andrea. *Haunted Hikes*. Santa Monica, California: Santa Monica Press, 2006.

Kuhn, Ferdinand. *Commodore Perry and the Opening of Japan*. New York, New York: Random House, 1955.

Leise, Cindy. "The Case of the Missing Monster." *Elyria Chronicle-Telegram*, June 12, 2005.

Martin, Jessie A. *The Beginnings and Tales of the Lake Erie Islands*. Detroit, Michigan: Harlo Press, 1990.

Lewis, Chad, and Terry Fisk. *The Wisconsin Road Guide to Haunted Locations.* Eau Claire, Wisconsin: Unexplained Research Publishing Company, 2004.

Ligibel, Ted, and Richard Wright. *Island Heritage.* Columbus, Ohio: Ohio State University Press, 1987.

Mitchell, Bruce. *The Australian Story and Its Background.* Melbourne, Australia: F.W. Cheshire, 1965.

Mollenkopf, Jim. *The Great Black Swamp.* Toledo, Ohio: Lake of the Cat Publishing, 1999.

Moran, C. "Torture Devices of the Old Convict Ships." *Modern Mechanics*, Sept., 1930.

Nash, Jay Robert. *Darkest Hours.* Chicago, Illinois: Nelson-Hall, 1976.

Newell, Amy L. *The Caves of Put-In Bay.* Put-In Bay, Ohio: Lake Erie Originals, 1995.

Oleszewski, Wes. *True Tales of Ghosts and Gales.* Gwinn, Michigan: Avery Color Studios, 2003.

Oleszewski, Wes. *Great Lakes Ghost Stories: Haunted Tales Past and Present.* Gwinn, Michigan: Avery Color Studios, 2004.

Payerchin, Richard. "Lake Erie monster returns." *Morning Journal of Lorain*, June 12, 2005.

Pennington, Rochelle. *The Historic Christmas Tree Ship: A True Story of Faith, Hope and Love.* Lomira, Wisconsin: Pathways Press, 2004.

Plowden, David. *End of an Era: The Last of the Great Lakes Steamboats.* New York, New York: W.W. Norton, 1992.

Ratigan, William. *Great Lakes Shipwrecks and Survivals.* Grand Rapids, Michigan: Eerdmans Publishing Company, 1977.

Renner, James. *It Came From Ohio...* Cleveland, Ohio: Gray & Company, 2012.

Schroeder, John H. *Matthew Calbraith Perry: Antebellum Sailor and Diplomat.* Annapolis, Maryland: Naval Institute Press, 2001.

Schumacher, Michael. *Mighty Fitz: The Sinking of the* Edmund Fitzgerald. New York, New York: Bloomsbury Publishing, 2005.

Scott, Beth and Michael Norman. *Haunted Heartland.* New York, New York: Warner Books, 1986.

Scott, Beth and Michael Norman. *Haunted America*. New York, New York: Tor Books, 1994.

Stone, David, and David Few. *The Lake Erie Quadrangle: Waters of Repose*. Erie, Pennsylvania: Erie County Historical Society, 1993.

Stonehouse, Frederick. *Great Lakes Crime*. Gwinn, Michigan: Avery Color Studios, 2004.

Stonehouse, Frederick. *Haunted Lakes*. Duluth, Minnesota: Lake Superior Port Cities, 1997.

Stonehouse, Frederick. Haunted Lakes II. Duluth, Minnesota: Lake Superior Port Cities, 2000.

Stonehouse, Frederick. *Haunted Lake Huron*. Duluth, Minnesota: Lake Superior Port Cities, 2007.

Stonehouse, Frederick. *Went Missing*. Gwinn, Michigan: Avery Color Studios, 1984 (Revised Edition).

Stonehouse, Frederick. *Steel on the Bottom*. Gwinn, Michigan: Avery Color Studios, 2006.

Stutz, Bruce. "Mysterious & Imperiled Creature of the Deep." *OnEarth*, Winter 2011/Spring 2012.

Swann, Brian, editor. *Coming to Light: Contemporary Translations of the Native Literatures of North America*. New York, New York: Random House, 1994.

Taylor, Troy, Adam Seltzer and Ken Melvoin-Berg. *Weird Chicago*. Alton, Illinois: Whitechapel Productions Press, 2008.

Thompson, Mark L. *Graveyard of the Lakes*. Detroit, Michigan: Wayne State University Press, 2000.

Trickey, Erick. "Wanted: South Bay Bessie." *Cleveland Magazine*, July, 2003.

Volgenau, Gerry. *Islands: Great Lakes Stories*. Ann Arbor, Michigan: Ann Arbor Media Group, 2005.

Wachter, Georgann and Michael. *Erie Wrecks West*. Avon Lake, Ohio: CorporateImpact, 2001.

Wachter, Georgann and Michael. *Erie Wrecks East*. Avon Lake, Ohio: CorporateImpact, 2ndrevised edition 2003.

Wachter, Georgann and Michael. *Erie Wrecks and Lights*. Avon Lake, Ohio: CorporateImpact, 2007.

Willis, James A, Andrew Henderson and Loren Coleman. *Weird Ohio*. New York, New York: Sterling Publishing Co., 2005.

Woodyard, Chris. *Haunted Ohio*. Dayton, Ohio: Kestrel Publications, 1991.

Woodyard, Chris. *Haunted Ohio II*. Dayton, Ohio: Kestrel Publications, 1992.

Woodyard, Chris. *Haunted Ohio III*. Dayton, Ohio: Kestrel Publications, 1995.

Woodyard, Chris. *Haunted Ohio IV*. Dayton, Ohio: Kestrel Publications, 1997.

Woodyard, Chris. *Haunted Ohio V*. Dayton, Ohio: Kestrel Publications, 2003.

Wright, Larry and Patricia. *Great Lakes Lighthouse Encyclopedia*. Erin, Ontario: The Boston Mills Press, 2006.

www.boatnerd.com

www.battleoflakeerie-bicentennial.com

www.chicagounbelievable.com

www.christmastreeship.com

www.cleveland.com.

www.johnmaynard.net

www.shipsuccess.com

Index